Housing, Poverty and Wealth in Ireland

HOUSING, POVERTY AND WEALTH IN IRELAND

by

Tony Fahey, Brian Nolan and Bertrand Maître

IPA
INSTITUTE OF PUBLIC
ADMINISTRATION

Combat Poverty
working for the prevention
and elimination of poverty   Agency

First published 2004
by the
Institute of Public Administration
57-61 Lansdowne Road
Dublin 4

and

Combat Poverty Agency
Bridgewater Centre
Conyngham Road
Islandbridge
Dublin 8

British Library Cataloguing in Publication Data

ISBN 1 904541 07 0

This study forms part of the Combat Poverty Agency Research Series in which it is No. 34.

The views expressed in this text are the author's own and not necessarily those of the Combat Poverty Agency.

Cover design by Red Dog Design Consultants, Dublin

Typeset by Typeform Repro, Dublin

Printed by Future Print, Ireland

Contents

List of Tables

List of Figures

FOREWORD

INTRODUCTION

Combat Poverty is a statutory body whose aim is to work for the prevention and elimination of poverty in Ireland. One of its strategic objectives is to achieve a greater understanding of poverty and social exclusion so as to inform policy on tackling poverty. Housing, a key determinant of living conditions, has been to the forefront of social and economic change in recent years in Ireland. However, little is known about the distributional effects of recent developments in the housing market, in particular for low-income groups. To address this deficit, Combat Poverty commissioned the Economic and Social Research Institute (ESRI) to carry out a pioneering study of housing poverty and wealth, with the following objectives:

- to outline patterns of housing tenure in an historical and comparative context;
- to assess the impact of housing costs on poverty risk; and
- to examine the distribution of housing as a form of wealth.

The study is based on analyses of survey data from the Household Budget Survey, the European Community Household Panel Survey and the Living in Ireland (LII) Survey and compliments an earlier Combat Poverty study that examined living conditions in the main component of Irish social housing – local authority housing estates.[1] This study builds on that earlier work by considering housing from a macro and a comparative perspective, focusing on housing tenure and on issues of housing poverty and wealth. This study also contributes to the debate about future directions in Irish social expenditure, which

---

1. Fahey, T. (ed.), *Social Housing in Ireland: A Study of Success, Failure and Lessons Learned* (Dublin: Oak Tree Press, in association with Combat Poverty Agency and Katharine Howard Foundation, 1999).

has been initiated in a recent Combat Poverty policy paper[2] that showed that the Irish welfare state lags behind the level of economic development achieved over the past decade, contributing to widening income differentials and macroeconomic inefficiency.

A key motivator in undertaking the study is that housing issues, while central to public policy debates in the last decade, have had a weak connection with government policies to tackle poverty. For instance, it was only in the revised National Anti-Poverty Strategy in 2002 that housing was included as a key objective.[3] Consideration of the links between housing and poverty is therefore only an emerging policy issue, where further research is needed to inform appropriate policy responses. This weak connection is especially apparent with regard to the provision of rent and mortgage supplements under the Supplementary Welfare Allowance. While expenditure has grown dramatically on these supplements in the private sector, it has done so without a clear understanding of their role in promoting access to housing.[4] Another example of this fragile policy framework is in relation to fuel poverty, where the state invests significant resources in supplementing heating costs in what is often fuel-inefficient housing, resulting in a low return in terms of housing warmth.[5]

POLICY CONTEXT

Housing has been a dominant feature of public policy in recent years, mainly on the basis of an increased demand for housing

2. Timonen, V., *Irish Social Expenditure in a Comparative International Context* (Dublin: Institute of Public Administration with Combat Poverty Agency, 2003).

3. Government of Ireland, *Building an Inclusive Society: Review of the National Anti-Poverty Strategy under the Programme for Prosperity and Fairness* (Dublin: Department of Social and Family Affairs, 2002).

4. Guerin, D., *Housing Income Support in the Private Rented Sector: A Survey of Recipients of SWA Rent Supplement* (Dublin: Combat Poverty Agency, 1999).

5. Healy, J., *Fuel Poverty and Policy in Ireland and the European Union*, Studies in Public Policy #12 (Dublin: The Policy Institute, Trinity College Dublin, in association with Combat Poverty Agency, 2004a).

(resulting from demographic pressures) and the associated escalation in housing costs. However, there has been little focus on the position of lower-income households in the housing market, in particular those in the private rented sector. More low-income households have entered this sector as traditional forms of social housing contracted. In addition, the private rented sector has borne the brunt of higher housing costs. These trends have had limited exposure in the policy debate, which has been dominated by the need to grow housing output, particularly home ownership. This narrow focus has facilitated a continued fall in the proportion of social housing relative to the total housing stock and an increase in waiting lists for those in need of social housing.

Concern about housing costs is reflected in the new policy concept of 'affordable private housing'. Action to increase housing output for this sector features prominently in the National Development Plan and more recently the social partnership programme, Sustaining Progress, which includes a special initiative to build 10,000 affordable homes using public land.[6]

Issues relating to housing provision also featured in the mid-term review of the National Development Plan. Housing has also featured in the work of the National Economic and Social Forum (NESF) and the National Economic and Social Council (NESC).[7] NESC has recognised the magnitude of the housing shortage problem, noting 'it is now widely accepted that housing shortages are one of the main constraints on Ireland's continued

---

6. However, available data on house completions under the Affordable Housing scheme indicates that the modest initial targets set under the Economic and Social Infrastructure Operational Programme are not being achieved. In fact, just 86 so-called affordable housing units were completed during 2000 compared to the targeted 1,000 homes. In 2001 there was some improvement on this figure, with 272 affordable units completed compared to the target of 1,000 dwellings. This data shows that just 17.9 per cent of the 2,000 affordable housing units were completed over the period 2000–1.

7. NESF, *Social and Affordable Housing and Accommodation: Building the Future* (Dublin: NESF, 2000) and NESC, *An Investment in Quality, Services and Enterprise* (Dublin: NESC, 2003).

economic growth and competitiveness, as well as a threat to social cohesion and quality of life.'[8] In response to this situation, NESC is currently undertaking a major review of housing policy.

The role of the Supplementary Welfare Allowance (SWA) scheme in supplementing housing costs has been the subject of a series of policy reviews, beginning in 1996. It has come under the microscope recently with the decision to restrict new applicants to those renting for a minimum of six months. In physical terms, some 60,000 homes were in receipt of rent allowances by the end of 2003. While there have been significant increases in SWA expenditure on housing needs, the number of recipients has not risen at the same rate. For instance, between 2000 and 2001 rent expenditure rose by a substantial 40.6 per cent, while the actual number of households receiving such subsidies rose by just 20.4 per cent. In addition, mortgage interest supplements rose by 20.8 per cent in monetary terms, while the number of recipients rose by 7 per cent.[9] This is due to a falling number of recipients of mortgage interest supplements among local authority dwellers.

Related to the role of SWA as a measure to reduce the severity of housing costs is the emerging policy debate about the impact of housing costs on quality of life and life satisfaction. A recent study by Healy (2003) indicated that Irish households perceive that they have particularly burdensome housing costs, above EU average levels.[10] One in five households nationally declared housing costs to be financially burdensome, compared to just 4.8 per cent in the Netherlands and 6.8 per cent in Denmark. The link between housing affordability problems and decreased quality of life is formally established in a forthcoming cross-country study.[11]

---

8. Quoted in NESC 2003, op cit., 259.
9. This data is derived from the 2002 Statistical Information on Social Welfare Services, published by the Department of Social and Family Affairs.
10. Healy, J.D., 'Housing conditions, energy efficiency, affordability and satisfaction with housing: a pan-European analysis', *Housing Studies*, 18/3 (2003), 409–24.
11. Healy, J.D., *Housing, Fuel Poverty and Health: A Pan-European Analysis* (Aldershot: Ashgate, 2004b).

Little attention has been paid to housing costs in the social rented sector, except to the extent that they might impact on incentives to take up employment and thus assist in locking households in a poverty trap. Yet this sector faces the highest risk of poverty. Also, this is an important source of debt problems for low-income households, as documented by the Money Advice and Budgetary Service (MABS).

Some €80.5 million was spent in 2002 on fuel allowances, making this measure the most heavily funded of all those covered under the 'free schemes' (27.2 per cent). Despite significant increases in state funding of this measure over the past decade (63 per cent in nominal terms), Irish households continue to suffer from relatively high levels of fuel poverty compared to their EU counterparts. One in ten Irish homes suffer chronic fuel poverty and the incidence is highest among low-income groups such as tenants, lone parents and the unemployed.[12] Some 20.9 per cent of tenants, the highest-risk group, are found to suffer chronic fuel poverty. Worryingly, this is the highest incidence found in this group among the whole of northern Europe. Such findings reiterate the need for continued and strengthened financial support for tenants in both the private and social rental sectors.

MAIN FINDINGS

The study reveals many new insights into the contemporary house market. Home ownership maintains its ascendancy, with Ireland continuing to demonstrate among the highest rates of home ownership in the EU at 80 per cent. Home ownership is pervasive across all income groups, with 60 per cent penetration among low-income households. Contrary to popular opinion, the study finds that, in general, home purchase has not become less affordable because of the countervailing impact of low real interest rates and higher incomes. Consequently, the dominance

---

12. Healy, J.D., *Fuel Poverty and Policy in Ireland and the European Union*, Studies in Public Policy #12 (Dublin: The Policy Institute, Trinity College Dublin, in association with Combat Poverty Agency, 2004a).

of owner occupation has actually increased in recent years, a period of housing growth. Thus, while housing output has increased by 153 per cent since 1993, the vast majority of housing completions went to the private market (97 per cent in 2001).[13]

The minority tenures – the social rented and private rented sectors – show contrasting trends. Social rented housing continues to decline, reflecting the privatisation of existing stock and its small share of new housing. The private rented sector is more dynamic, but from a small base. These two segments of the housing market have come under severe pressure, as issues of housing affordability are concentrated in the private rented sector. Housing costs increase the poverty risk of households in the private rented sector, while diminishing those in owner occupation. Overall, poverty rates are highest among local authority tenants. Falling levels of local authority completions and increased demand have led to a dramatic rise in waiting lists, which is one of the factors that has led to rising levels of homelessness.

Four-fifths of households have some form of housing wealth, i.e. they are homeowners and the market value of their house is greater than the outstanding debt. The distribution of home ownership is apparent across the income schedule, with the poorest 20 per cent of households holding 15 per cent of total net housing wealth. A key mechanism for distributing housing wealth among low-income households is tenant purchase. On the other hand, low-income households that are not home-owners are doubly disadvantaged, especially if in the high-rent private rented sector. It is among this grouping that housing poverty is concentrated.

POLICY RESPONSE

Combat Poverty is of the view that access to good-quality, affordable housing should be a fundamental goal of public

---

13. Griffen, N., 'Current Housing Supply Policy and its Future Direction', paper presented to Access to Housing: Affordability, Policy and Development Issues, Dublin, September 2002.

policy and is central to policy to tackle poverty. Overall housing policy should be adjusted to take account of new social trends, with a greater emphasis on 'affordable rental housing' as a response to the housing needs of low-income, younger and transitional households. Policy recommendations may be grouped into three broad groups: those specific to the private rental sector, those pertinent to social and affordable housing and those with implications for owner occupiers.

Private and Social Rental Sectors

There should be increased investment in good-quality social and private rental housing, using a range of housing providers (public, private, non-governmental) so that the rental sector increases its proportionate share of the national dwelling stock. The priority given to the affordable housing initiative in Sustaining Progress is beneficial and future initiatives could focus on the private rental sector in an effort to alleviate chronic house shortages, especially among low-income and younger households. An increase in the demand for rented dwellings could also act as a deflationary pulse in the heated owner-occupier sector.

On the demand side, a review should be undertaken with regard to the role of rental subsidies, such as tax relief and SWA rent supplements, as supports for addressing housing affordability in the private rented sector. The findings in this report on affordability in this sector are particularly salient and it is clear that subvention in the private rental sector through SWA measures is crucial to the ability of low-income households to afford this accommodation.[14]

While rental supplements may be considered satisfactory short-term measures to reduce the risk of housing poverty, it is prudent that such approaches be supplemented by long-term supply measures aimed at addressing demographic pressures. In this regard, increasing the number of 'affordable housing' units and increasing the pool of social housing should be a priority for housing policy. Combat Poverty feels that rental subsidies are not a particularly efficient means of improving access to housing, as evidence indicates that in the absence of an increasing (or flexible) supply of rental accommodation, this measure actually pushes up the price of rents in the private rental sector; in effect, the subsidy is passed on to landlords who then reap the monetary benefits.

Existing tax incentives for the private rented sector should be concentrated on the lower (affordable) end of the private rental sector, e.g. similar to the student accommodation initiative. A key point here is that incentives need to be put in place to encourage investors to rent out properties so that there is a supply shift in the private rental sector. Such an increase should lead to improved affordability (and desirability) of rental accommodation. A proviso here is that regulatory measures are safeguarded to ensure that such accommodation satisfies requirements of satisfactory living conditions.

Social Housing

The study recommends that the supply of social housing units be increased considerably. Less than 10 per cent of new house completions are social housing, compared with 35 per cent in the 1970s. Some commentators may point to the 2000 Economic and Social Infrastructure Operational Programme and to the social and affordable housing targets contained within that initiative. Yet these targets are modest compared with the scale of the demand-side pressures that are currently facing the housing market and are equally modest when compared with social housing schemes undertaken hitherto in Ireland.

In the local authority housing segment there may be a case for the expansion of 'fuzzy tenures', where tenants part own, part rent.[15] This could assist in the creation of an improved continuum of housing tenures, producing a more diverse supply

14. It should be noted that as a result of the recent review of SWA allowances in the 2004 budget, there is now 'restricted entry' into the SWA rent allowance (households must be renting for six months before they are entitled to draw down the allowance). This change has risen out of the increasing numbers claiming the rent allowance in recent years (60,000 homes in 2003).

15. Hills, J., 'Inclusion or exclusion? The role of housing subsidies and benefits', *Urban Studies*, 38/11 (2001), 1087–92.

of affordable housing. Some analysts have suggested that renting to middle-income residents could cross-subsidise the costs of providing housing for poorer households.[16] Such a measure is likely to be highly economically efficient while also improving the affordability of housing costs to middle-income households, which data indicates are finding it increasingly difficult to enter into the property market. In addition, housing costs for the social rented sector need to be reviewed in light of the high risk of poverty among tenants and the propensity to indebtedness. An attendant issue is the so-called 'right to buy' or 'tenant purchase' scheme, which has been in existence for many years. This has clear benefits, but it also has implications in regards to restricting the supply of units in the social housing sector. Striking the correct balance here is difficult, which emphasises the need for increased investment in social and affordable housing initiatives.

There is also scope for a substantial expansion of non-profit housing associations.[17] Higher non-profit housing completions in 2000 and 2001 were targeted in the Economic and Social Infrastructural Operational Programme, yet targets in this sector are small relative to the entire social housing projections under this programme. A vibrant voluntary housing sector would create competition and dampen rents and speculation, leading to improved affordability and increased desirability.[18]

Furthermore, it is important that new social and affordable housing schemes are planned in such a way that access to services is prioritised. Good-quality infrastructure and public services are fundamental issues often overlooked in the planning process.

---

16. MacLaran, A., 'Middle class social housing: insanity or progress?', *Cornerstone: Magazine of the Homeless Initiative*, 5 (April 2000).

17. Mullins, D., Rhodes, M.L. and Williamson, A., *Non-Profit Housing Organisations in Ireland, North and South* (Belfast: Northern Ireland Housing Executive, 2003).

18. Drudy, P.J. and Punch, M., 'Housing models, housing rights: a framework for discussion', in M. Punch and L. Buchanan (eds), *Housing Rights: A New Approach?* (Dublin: Threshold, 2003), 1–14.

Owner Occupiers

The study shows that 78 per cent of Irish households have some net wealth in the form of housing. The scope for taxing housing as a form of wealth needs to be reconsidered in light of these findings. However, it is recognised that such a move may be highly contentious and politically difficult. In the short term, it is recommended that the growth of second homes as a form of housing wealth should be prioritised from a tax perspective.

Combat Poverty also believes that it would be prudent to review regulatory measures governing banks and financial institutions to ascertain the viability and suitability of minimal-deposit mortgage lending, where as much as 100 per cent of the house value may be obtained. Although owner occupiers are no more burdened now than historically in terms of monthly mortgage repayments as a proportion of net household disposable income, the increasing size (in real and proportionate terms) of mortgages could become cause for serious concern under less favourable macroeconomic conditions. Low- or middle-income households currently financially stretched and with large mortgages may end up being faced with large increases in monthly repayments in situations of interest rate variations instigated by the European Central Bank and over which Irish policymakers have little control.

A missing factor in this study is the quality of housing. In this regard, the recently published Irish National Survey of Housing Quality is a significant step in the right direction towards filling an important and often overlooked information gap, that of housing quality.[19] It is clear from a recently conducted pan-EU study that Ireland suffers from varying housing conditions; overcrowding and poor thermal efficiency are particularly prevalent.[20] Further work is required to investigate this issue, especially in the private rented sector, so that a socio-economic

19. Watson, D. and Williams, J., *Irish National Survey of Housing Quality 2001–2002* (Dublin: ESRI, 2003).
20. Healy, J.D., 'Housing conditions, energy efficiency, affordability and satisfaction with housing: a pan-European analysis', *Housing Studies*, 18/3 (2003), 409–24.

profile of housing conditions can highlight those households most vulnerable to sub-standard housing conditions. Regulatory measures must be maintained and strengthened to monitor the housing conditions in the private rental sector, which is particularly susceptible to adverse and varying living conditions.

CONCLUSION

Housing policy has largely neglected issues of housing poverty and wealth. It is imperative that the anti-poverty dimension of housing policy is strengthened, building on the new departure signalled in the National Anti-Poverty Strategy. The role of housing as a widespread source of wealth should also be reconsidered in the context of promoting social equity.

EXECUTIVE SUMMARY

Rapid increases in house prices in recent years have raised concerns about the affordability of housing for home buyers, with much attention being focused on the circumstances of first-time buyers. On the other hand, those who already own their homes have seen their housing assets rise in value and tenants in the private rented sector have experienced sharp rises in rents. Taken together, these developments have had complex consequences for inequalities in income and living standards, for the risk of poverty across tenure categories and for the distribution of wealth. The purpose of this study is to examine these issues from an anti-poverty perspective, taking account of the historical and comparative context in which they arise. Given the dominance of home ownership in the Irish housing system, the study focuses in particular on the growth of owner occupation in Ireland. It examines household spending on home purchase compared to other types of housing tenure, assesses the effect of that spending on living standards and household poverty, outlines the wealth distribution effects of home ownership and draws out implications for policy. The study is based on existing data, drawn mainly from the Household Budget Surveys for various years, the Living in Ireland (LII) Survey 2000 and the European Community Household Budget Survey 1996.

HISTORICAL BACKGROUND

Over 80 per cent of Irish householders own their homes, one of the highest rates of home ownership in the EU. The historical origins of this high home ownership level can be traced back to the rural land reforms of the early twentieth century and the policy of tenant purchase of local authority housing, which was initiated in the 1930s based on land reform precedents. A long and complex tradition of grant giving and fiscal supports for owner occupation of housing has also played an important role.

Some of these supports – especially mortgage interest relief – were reduced during the 1990s. However, in the face of falling interest rates, a booming economy and a growing young-adult population, these reductions in fiscal subsidy had little dampening effect on house price rises over the past ten years. Since the 1960s, interest rates have been low for long periods and periodic bouts of general price and wage inflation have regularly eroded the value of mortgage debt. These factors have greatly aided home purchase for owner occupation and have added to the incentive for householders to buy rather than rent their homes.

PRESENT TENURE PATTERNS

The number of owner-occupied dwellings in Ireland has doubled over the past three decades and has grown as a share of the total housing stock. The social rented sector has declined in relative terms, initially on account of tenant purchase of local authority housing and more recently because of the relatively small extent of new social housing construction. The relative size of the private rented sector also shrank until the 1990s, reflecting the longstanding bias in the housing system towards home ownership. Although the private rented sector appears to have increased marginally in relative size over the last decade it is still small by international standards, particularly given that Ireland has a large young-adult population, among whom demand for the kind of flexible, easy-access accommodation offered by the private rented sector would be expected to be high.

The high overall level of home ownership means that owner occupation is high throughout the income distribution and the social class hierarchy. About 60 per cent of those in the bottom one-fifth of the income distribution are owner occupiers and the same is true of those in the unskilled manual social class. The proportion of owner occupiers who have a mortgage declines with age, so that among those aged 65 or over about 80 per cent own their dwellings without any associated mortgage.

PRICES AND AGGREGATE AFFORDABILITY OF HOUSE PURCHASE

House prices have risen sharply since the mid-1990s, but falling interest rates have served to offset the impact on the cost of servicing mortgage debt. As a result, aggregate indicators showed no consistent worsening in the burden of mortgage payments relative to household income during the house price boom of the 1990s. House purchasers, however, may be vulnerable to an increase in interest rates. The gap between house prices and average incomes also makes it difficult for house buyers to accumulate the required deposit, though it is not clear that this problem is of significantly greater proportions now than at other times in the past.

HOUSEHOLD EXPENDITURE ON HOUSING

Household-level data on households' weekly spending patterns indicates that the largest increases in household expenditures on housing since the 1980s have occurred in the private rented sector. By 1999–2000, the average private rent was almost three times greater than it had been in 1987 in real terms, while the share of household expenditure absorbed by rent among private tenants had increased 1.7 times (from 12.5 per cent to 21 per cent of household expenditure). Among those purchasing for owner occupation, mortgage payments increased in absolute terms by 42 per cent between 1987 and 1999–2000, but the share of household expenditure absorbed by mortgage payments remained more or less stable at around 10 per cent of household expenditure. Even among new entrants to the housing market, the increase in mortgage burdens was limited. Younger house purchasers devoted only a marginally higher share of their total spending to mortgage payments in 1999–2000 than they had in 1994–5 and still had mortgage payment burdens that were reasonably manageable and were lower (relative to household income) than the rent burdens faced by private renters. Though house prices in Dublin are higher than in other parts of the country, the most serious negative effect on housing expenditures and housing affordability in the Dublin area is evident among private renters rather than among those purchasing their homes. For those in social rented accommodation, housing expenditures have been low and stable over the long term, have shown little change in recent years and differ little between urban and rural areas.

These developments mean that a large gap has opened up between the burden of housing expenditures for private renters and mortgage purchasers. In 1987, private rents and mortgage payments were at similar levels, both in absolute amounts and as a share of household expenditure. Yet by 1999–2000, the average private rent was 1.7 times the average mortgage payment in absolute amounts and was 2.2 times the average mortgage payment as a share of total household expenditure.

Consequently, the most serious affordability problems found in the Irish housing system at present have arisen in the private rented sector and are most severe in Dublin. If we take expenditures on rent or mortgage payments that exceed 35 per cent of household expenditure as an indicator of likely financial strain arising from housing costs (a benchmark that is widely used for this purpose), then about one in five private renting households experienced such strain in 1999–2000, while only 1 per cent of home purchasers did so. In Dublin, more than one in four private renters had rents exceeding the 35 per cent affordability threshold, while only 1.2 per cent of home purchases had mortgage payments above that level. Even among house purchasers in the earliest stages of the family cycle, where mortgage burdens were heaviest, less than 5 per cent had mortgage payments that exceeded the 35 per cent threshold – a far lower incidence of financial pressures arising from housing costs than was found in the private rented sector. Though private rents seem to have reached a plateau in 2002 and may have declined since then, the extent of the decline is unlikely to have been great enough to cancel out prior increases or to reduce the concentration of housing affordability problems in the private rented sector just pointed to.

HOUSING EXPENDITURE IN COMPARATIVE PERSPECTIVE

Irish households in general spend a lower share of their incomes on rent and mortgages than the average for the EU, partly because almost half of Irish householders are outright home-owners and so have zero rent or mortgage costs. However, even among homeowners with mortgages, mortgage payments in Ireland, which on average account for about 10 per cent of weekly expenditure among those households, are also moderately low by EU standards. Among younger house purchasers such payments rise to almost 20 per cent of household expenditure on average, which is closer to the EU mean. Social rents are particularly low in Ireland, at less than 8 per cent of household expenditure. In the case of private renters, the share of household spending going on rent is of the order of 20 per cent, which is similar to the levels seen in many other EU countries. Thus, although private rents in Ireland are now more burdensome on private renting households than are mortgage payments among home purchasers, they are not particularly high, relative to household income, compared with the rest of the EU.

HOUSING EXPENDITURE AND POVERTY

The differing levels of spending on housing across tenures means that some categories of households have a lower share of their incomes available for non-housing consumption than others and have a correspondingly higher risk of falling below minimum acceptable levels in these aspects of living standards. Tenants in the private rented sector are particularly at risk in this regard, since their housing expenditures are especially high. An adjusted measure of poverty that takes crude account of the burden of rent and mortgage payments shows a substantially higher risk of poverty among private tenants than is shown by conventional poverty measures and a lower risk of poverty among outright homeowners. Other tenure categories show little change in risk of poverty using this adjusted poverty measure and the overall level of poverty is unchanged. There is an increase in risk of poverty for lone parents and for the unemployed (who are prominent in the private rented sector), but a significant decline for the elderly, who are most likely to own their houses outright. Non-monetary indicators of deprivation also indicate that private renters are particularly prone to economic hardship, thus adding to the evidence that affordability problems in housing are most likely to be severe and to lead to real difficulties in living standards in the private rented sector.

THE DISTRIBUTION OF HOUSING WEALTH

Ownership of wealth is an additional aspect of households' command over material resources. About 78 per cent of Irish households have some net wealth in the form of housing, that is, they are owner occupiers and the market value of their house is greater than the outstanding debt on their mortgage. This wide distribution of housing wealth means that the proportion that are homeowners and their average house value are quite high, even towards the bottom of the income distribution. Households in the bottom one-fifth of the income distribution hold 15 per cent of total net housing wealth compared to only 7 per cent of total income, while households in the top one-fifth of the income distribution hold 25 per cent of housing wealth compared to 41 per cent of income. The elderly, whose incomes are low, have a particularly high proportion of housing wealth. Thus, although ownership of housing wealth is unevenly distributed, it runs counter to inequalities in income to some degree and therefore has a certain balancing effect on the overall distribution of resources. However, some of those on low incomes own no housing wealth. If they are in the private rented sector and facing high rents they are likely to be disadvantaged both in income available for non-housing purposes and in wealth.

A comparison between 1994 and 2000 suggests that the house price boom did not have a substantial impact on the overall distribution of net housing wealth over the income distribution. The mean net value of housing as an asset rose throughout the distribution, though slightly faster towards the top of the income distribution. On the other hand, the increase in the home ownership rate was concentrated in the bottom half of the distribution. As a result, the share of total net housing wealth held by the bottom one-fifth or two-fifths of the income distribution changed little between the mid-1990s and 2000.

CONCERNS FOR POLICY

The official objective of Irish housing policy is 'to enable every household to have available an affordable dwelling of good quality, suited to its needs, in a good environment and, as far as possible, at the tenure of its choice' (see www.environ.ie under 'Housing Policy'). This study identifies concerns relating to two elements of this objective – affordability of dwellings and tenure choice.

A key finding of the study is that problems regarding the affordability of dwellings are most severe in the private rented sector and have the greatest impact from a poverty perspective in that sector. Private sector tenants are burdened with higher housing expenditures than any other tenure category and experience considerable financial strain as a result. In contrast, among those purchasing for home ownership, financial strain arising from mortgage expenditures is less widely present and has not greatly increased over time. This is as true of younger households who entered the housing market during the house price boom of the late 1990s as it is of older households. The main concern for recent entrants to the housing market arises from the possibility of changing circumstances in the future, such as a rise in interest rates or increases in unemployment, and the strain such changes could cause rather than from the current burden of mortgage expenditures.

In addition, there is a concern for those who have been unable to get a foothold on the house purchase ladder on account of the entry barriers posed by deposit requirements and other entry costs. It is by no means clear that the proportion of young households that are in this situation is any greater than at other points in the past, keeping in mind that large minorities of households always found it difficult or impossible to enter the house purchase market at early stages in the family cycle. Rather, the problems of households on the margins of house purchase today point to a second policy concern arising from the present study – the question of tenure choice and in particular the limited range of tenure options available to those who either do not want to enter owner occupation or who are unable to make the transition across the initial entry threshold into house purchase.

The key issue here is that housing options for households in these circumstances have narrowed over time. Consequently, they are now constrained to rely more heavily on home purchase as a means of providing themselves with accommodation than was the case in the past. This narrowing of housing options has arisen from three developments. The first is the reduction in new social housing construction from levels in the range of 20–35 per cent of total new housing construction, which it attained in the 1970s and 1980s, to less than 10 per cent today. This means that a large category of low-income households that formerly would have turned to social rental housing as their first option (usually with an option to buy through tenant purchase at a later stage in the family cycle) must now look elsewhere.

A second development is that private rented accommodation has become much more expensive in absolute terms and relative to the cost of accommodation in other tenures. This development has priced many low-income households out of the private rental market, while other potential private renters have been channelled towards home purchase even when that option might be less than optimal for them in their circumstances. Welfare-dependent households that seek accommodation in the private rented sector can obtain welfare support towards their rental costs in the form of rent allowances under the Supplementary Welfare Allowance scheme, but such supports are not available to low-income households that are outside the welfare net.

The third, and less important, reduction in housing options is the virtual disappearance of the public sector mortgages (provided by local authorities and the Housing Finance Agency) as a means of access to house purchase for low-income households. In the 1970s and 1980s, public sector mortgages generally accounted for about a quarter of the total mortgage market and were targeted towards those who would be unable to meet the financial requirements needed to obtain private sector mortgages. Today this source of mortgage credit accounts for only a fraction of 1 per cent of the total mortgage market, so that those who formerly would have constituted the clientele for this kind of house purchase credit must now look to private sector lending agencies. Private sector mortgages are now available in greater abundance, on easier terms and at lower nominal interest rates than was the case in the past, so the decline of public sector mortgages is less significant than it otherwise might have been. However, it represents a housing option that was widespread in the past but which has all but disappeared today.

These developments mean that a reasonably diverse set of housing options available to low-income households prior to the 1990s has become narrowed to a more limited range of possibilities at present. New households must either buy their homes or struggle to obtain alternatives that have become either very scarce (social housing) or both scarce and expensive (private renting). Households not requiring the long-term accommodation associated with owner occupation (such as young adults, migrants or those departing the family home) might formerly have preferred to rent their accommodation but are now directed into attempting to buy as a way of avoiding high rents, thus adding to the pressure on the house purchase market while failing to achieve tenure choice. These patterns would suggest that what is distinctive about the housing market in Ireland in recent times is not that so few newly formed households are able to afford house purchase, but rather that so many are expected to make this large housing acquisition with such immediacy in the early stages of household formation or as a precondition for other major life cycle transitions.

Policy Recommendations

The policy recommendations arising from these findings are as follows.

1. Irish housing policy should modify the present emphasis on home ownership as a housing solution and place greater emphasis on rental housing options, especially for those on low incomes, in the young-adult stages of the life cycle and in other forms of transitional household.

2. The private and social rented sectors need to be expanded, both in absolute terms and as a proportion of the housing stock. It is open to question what the balance between social and private rented accommodation in an expanded rental sector should be or whether intermediate kinds of rental tenure might be introduced to create a continuum between the two. The key point is that the rental sector should be larger and more diverse in the rent levels and tenure arrangements it offers to households than it is at present.

3. The goal of restraining price increases and promoting the affordability of housing destined for owner occupation is laudable in itself, but should not be pursued at the expense of either the private or social rented sectors. Fiscal or other measures that were introduced in the past in order to deter 'investors' from purchasing housing should not be repeated.

4. A concept of 'affordable housing' emerged in Irish housing policy in the 1990s which was applied solely to housing being purchased for owner occupation and made no reference to the circumstances of private renters. This concept now exerts some influence (see point following), but is excessively narrow, fails to address the most serious affordability problems in the Irish housing system and is at odds with the tenure-neutral goal of affordability that is included in the official objective of Irish housing policy. It therefore should be avoided in future policy development and a return should be made to the broader concept of affordability that underlies the overall objective of Irish housing policy.

5. The 10,000 additional housing units proposed under the 'affordable housing initiative' set out in the most recent national agreement, Sustaining Progress (2003), are to be directed to those on low incomes purchasing for owner occupation. A valid rationale for restricting the initiative in this way to those purchasing for owner occupation is hard to detect. A strong case could be made that an affordable housing initiative of this kind should be directed at least in equal measure, and perhaps even primarily, at the rental sector and that it should be delivered in such a way as to increase the supply of rental housing and reduce the rent burdens experienced by private sector tenants. It is beyond the scope of this study to suggest how the initiative might be designed to achieve these ends (an issue dealt with extensively by the Report of the Commission on the Private Rented Residential Sector 2000), but rather the point is to emphasise the seriousness of the need which arises in this area and the requirement that housing policy treat this need as a priority.

6. Rent allowances provided under the Supplementary Welfare Allowances scheme as a support for housing costs to welfare-dependent tenants in the private rented sector play an important role in alleviating housing affordability problems in that sector. However, this form of housing support has not been designed as a comprehensive solution to such affordability problems, nor has it been located within a comprehensive strategy to promote a vibrant, diverse private rental sector. On its own, therefore, it is inadequate as a response to problems in the sector and needs to be re-examined and redesigned as an element of a broader strategy.

INTRODUCTION

Recent years have seen dramatic developments in the Irish housing market. Most attention has been directed at the unprecedented increase in house prices that took place after the onset of the economic boom in the mid-1990s, which gave rise to concerns about the affordability of home purchase, particularly for first-time buyers. A series of reports commissioned by the government in the late 1990s (the three Bacon Reports) made recommendations on how the upward movement in house prices might be halted and how purchase for owner occupation might be made more affordable (Bacon and Associates 1998, 1999, 2000), many of which were acted upon (Department of the Environment and Local Government 1998, 1999, 2000a). Other consequences of the changing housing market received less attention, such as the increase in the value of housing assets among existing homeowners and the effect of housing scarcity and rising housing values in pushing up rent levels in the private rented sector. Taken together, these developments had complex consequences for the inequalities in incomes, living standards, the risk of poverty and the distribution of wealth in Ireland. Depending on the tenure circumstances and income levels of households, the share of household resources absorbed by spending on housing may have risen, fallen or stayed the same, while the relative position of households in the national distribution of housing wealth may similarly have altered in any direction. Rising housing costs might have driven certain categories of households into relative poverty, but again the extent of that risk differed across tenures and income categories.

Little detailed analysis has so far been carried out on these distributional consequences or on the long-term trends within which they might be located and understood. The purpose of this study, commissioned by the Combat Poverty Agency, is to address these gaps in knowledge from an anti-poverty point of view, taking particular account of the consequences of the dominance of home ownership in Irish housing patterns and in the policy concerns of successive governments. The objectives of the study are to:

- describe Ireland's patterns of home ownership and housing tenure in a historical and comparative context and assess how policy has influenced these trends;
- investigate the extent to which spending on housing affects living standards and in particular household poverty;
- look at how the distribution of wealth in the form of housing has been affected by recent developments; and
- identify the policy implications arising from the findings.

The study is based on a number of existing data sources. Trend data on expenditure on housing is drawn from Household Budget Surveys (HBS) carried out by the Central Statistics Office (CSO) over the period 1973 to 1999–2000. Micro-data files made available by the CSO from this source are used for the 1994–5 and 1999–2000 rounds of the HBS, while published data is used for the 1973, 1980 and 1987 rounds. Comparative data on housing tenure and housing expenditures in the EU are taken from the 1996 wave of the European Community Household Panel Survey (ECHP), which is a harmonised, longitudinal survey established by Eurostat in 1994 and conducted annually in 14 EU countries based on large samples of households (Sweden is the member state which does not take part in the survey). Its main purpose is to collect data on incomes, living standards and related aspects of material well-being in the participating countries (for a full description see Eurostat 2001 and Watson 2003). The 1996 wave of the ECHP is used here, as it was the most recent available wave containing comprehensive data on housing tenure and housing expenditures. The national version of the ECHP in Ireland is known as the Living in Ireland (LII) survey, which is carried out by the ESRI in co-ordination with Eurostat (Layte et al. 2001; Nolan et al. 2002). As well as the core ECHP data the LII collects a range of additional variables, of which some (especially those relating to housing wealth) are particularly relevant to the present study. The LII's 2000 wave is used here to examine the implications of present housing patterns for poverty and the distribution of housing wealth in Ireland. Other sources are used for incidental purposes in the course of the study and these are indicated as they arise.

The study is structured as follows: reflecting the importance of home ownership in the Irish housing system, we begin by looking at how the level of home ownership in Ireland has evolved over time, the social profile of those in owner occupation, how Irish levels of home ownership compare with those of other countries and recent trends in house prices. We then examine the role public policy has played over a long period in influencing patterns of housing tenure in Ireland. Household spending on housing and how it varies across tenure types and household characteristics is then analysed in some depth and is placed in international perspective by means of comparisons with other European Union countries. We then turn to an assessment of the extent and nature of the direct impact of spending on housing on household poverty. The distribution of wealth in the form of housing and how that has evolved over recent years is then analysed. Finally, the main findings of the study are brought together and the implications for policy are assessed.

AUTHORS

PROFESSOR TONY FAHEY

Tony Fahey has a PhD in sociology from the University of Illinois at Champaign-Urbana in the USA. He is currently a Research Professor in the ESRI.

PROFESSOR BRIAN NOLAN

Brian Nolan obtained a PhD in economics from the London School of Economics and is currently a Research Professor in the ESRI.

BERTRAND MAÎTRE

Bertrand Maître is a Research Analyst at the ESRI. He has a Master's degree in Economics from the University of La Sorbonne, Paris.

Chapter 1

THE EVOLUTION OF HOME OWNERSHIP AND HOUSE PRICES IN IRELAND

1.1 INTRODUCTION

Ireland's particular pattern of home ownership has deep historical roots, so it is useful to begin by sketching how the level of home ownership in Ireland arrived at its current position. This chapter then seeks to put Ireland's pattern of housing tenure in comparative context by looking at how it differs from other European Union countries. Finally, since much of the attention being directed at housing in recent years arises from the dramatic rate of increase in house prices, the evolution of house prices and some associated trends are also described.

1.2 TRENDS IN HOUSING TENURE OVER TIME IN IRELAND

Table 1.1 sets out the evolution of tenure patterns in Ireland since 1946, the first year for which comprehensive tenure data is available. In 1946 the overall home ownership rate was 53 per cent. Home ownership was particularly high in rural areas at 69 per cent, reflecting the impact of land reform over the previous half century. Urban home ownership, on the other hand, was only 23 per cent.

Since 1946 the overall home ownership rate has risen from 52.6 per cent to its present position above 80 per cent. In rural areas about 88 per cent now own their homes, with much of this increase having already taken place by 1971. In urban areas the increase was more recent and more pronounced, with home ownership reaching 73 per cent by 1991.

In the three decades since 1971 the housing stock has grown by 68 per cent, from 726,400 units to 1.22 million units, while the proportion of that stock which was owner occupied grew from 69 per cent to 82 per cent. In absolute terms this entailed a doubling of the stock of owner-occupied housing, from 500,000 to 1 million units.

The growth of home ownership over recent decades has been accompanied by a decline in both the private and social rented sectors (the latter now consists of both local authority housing and housing provided by voluntary housing associations). Both of these sectors were already modest in size in 1961, accounting for 18 per cent and 17 per cent of the total housing stock, respectively. Thereafter the social rented sector declined steadily in relative terms, falling below 8 per cent of the total in 1999–2000 (for an account of this decline and the reasons behind it see Fahey 1999). At first glace this decline would appear to be anomalous since the output of new local authority rental housing was large in this period, exceeding 30 per cent of new house construction in the early 1970s and remaining above 20 per cent until cutbacks in social housing expenditure were introduced in 1987 (Figure 1.1). Following fiscal retrenchment in 1987, social housing construction fell to below 10 per cent of the total new construction and has not recovered to the much higher levels of the 1970s since then.

The decline in the relative size of the social housing sector, even during periods of high levels of new social housing construction, is accounted for by tenant purchase of existing local authority housing. Tenant purchase, discussed in further detail below, was first introduced on a large scale in the 1930s and grew rapidly in the aftermath of expanded arrangements provided for in the 1966 Housing Act. Consequently, in the 1970s and 1980s existing local authority housing was being sold to tenants as fast as new local authority housing was being built, resulting in stability in the total numbers of dwellings in local authority ownership and a decline in the relative size of the local authority stock. All these trends together have led to a 'residualisation' of local authority housing, i.e. its concentration on a smaller population of poorer households, which is evident in the trends for this sector that are examined below (see also Housing Unit 2002; O'Connell and Fahey 1999).

Table 1.1 Dwellings by type of tenure in Ireland (per cent), 1946–2000

	1946	1961	1971	1981	1991	1999–2000
Owner occupied	52.6	59.8	68.8	74.4	79.3	82
Rural	69.3	77.4	85.5	85.6	87.8	
Urban	23.2	38.0	52.5	65.6	73.1	
Social housing	42.7	18.4	15.5	12.5	9.7	8
Private rented		17.2	13.3	10.1	8.0	9
Total	100	100	100	100	100	100
Total no. of dwellings (000s)	662.6	676.4	726.4	896.1	1,019.7	1,220.9

Note: Data for 1946 does not distinguish between private and social renting.
Source: Censuses of Population 1946–1991; Household Budget Survey 1999–2000

The private rented sector has also declined in relative size since 1961, falling to only 8 per cent of the total housing stock in 1991. This decline was the counterpart of the growth in home ownership and can be interpreted largely as a side effect of factors promoting that growth (Department of the Environment and Local Government 2000a; McCashin 2000). After 1991 this sector increased marginally as a proportion of the total, reaching 9 per cent of the total housing stock according to estimates based on the 1999–2000 Household Budget Survey.[1] The increase in the

---

1. In the absence of the comprehensive count of households by tenure that will become available when the results of the 2002 Census are published, there is some uncertainty about the exact size of the private rented sector. The Report of the Commission on the Private Rented Sector (2000: 8) gave an estimate of 131,000 households in the sector in 1997, based on Labour Force Survey (LFS) data on housing tenure for that year. This was the equivalent of 11 per cent of all households and implied that the private rented sector was growing rapidly, with a 62 per cent increase since 1991.

Figure 1.1 Social housing construction as percentage of all housing construction, 1970–2002

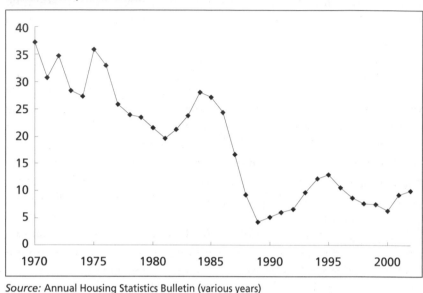

Source: Annual Housing Statistics Bulletin (various years)

private rented sector in the 1990s caused it to become slightly larger than the social rented sector, the first time this had occurred since the rapid expansion of the social rented sector in the 1940s and 1950s. The changing relative size of these two sectors in the 1990s must be interpreted in light of the decline in new social housing construction in the late 1980s coupled with the rapid growth of public expenditure on rent allowances under the Supplementary Welfare Allowances (SWA) scheme

However, the module on housing included in the CSO's 1998 Quarterly National Household Survey (QNHS) 3rd Quarter produced an estimate of 199,300 households in the private and social rented sectors combined, which, given that there are over 100,000 households in the social sector alone, would imply that the private rented sector may have comprised only around 100,000 households at that time. This suggests only slight growth in the relative size of the private rented sector since 1991. The estimate based on the 1999–2000 Household Budget Survey quoted in Table 1.1 above is more consistent with the QNHS estimate of 1998 than the LFS estimate of 1997, but only the 2002 Census results will clarify which estimate is closest to reality.

over the same period.[2] The growth in rent allowances meant that the private rented sector took on a new quasi-social housing role during the 1990s (Fahey and Watson 1995: 166–84) and the impact of this role on housing expenditure in the sector is an issue we will return to in due course.

Owning one's home does not necessarily mean that the household's net wealth includes the full market value of the house, since there may be associated borrowings used to finance the purchase. However, the long history of relatively high home ownership in Ireland also means that many homes are in fact now debt free, despite the rapid growth in home building and new house purchase over recent decades. Table 1.2 shows the proportion of households that were owner occupied with and without a mortgage from the early 1970s to 1999–2000. In the early 1970s, less than one in four dwellings and one in three owner occupiers, about 161,000 in number, held mortgages. An increasing recourse to mortgage financing as a way of accessing housing occurred during the 1970s and 1980s so that by 1991, 41 per cent of dwellings – over 413,000 – and over half of all owner occupiers had mortgages. (These figures include former local authority tenants who were acquiring their houses through tenant purchase, numbering 65,000 in 1991.) By 1999–2000 the earlier expansion of widespread mortgage financing had begun to mature, yielding a growing proportion of homeowners who had cleared their mortgage debt. Outright owner occupiers free of mortgage debt rose from 38 per cent of all householders in 1991 to 47 per cent in 1999–2000. This restored the relative position that had prevailed prior to the mortgage boom of the 1970s and 1980s, where about 55 per cent of owner-occupied dwellings were held without a mortgage.

The implication of these patterns is that despite the rapid increase in the housing stock in the 1990s, households taking out new mortgages at the beginning of the house purchase cycle were outnumbered by those emerging at the other end having

---

2. Expenditure on such allowances expanded 23-fold between 1989 and 2001, that is, from €7.75 million (£6.1 million) in 1989 to €179.4 million in 2001.

cleared their existing mortgages. The relative significance of mortgage holding as an aspect of overall tenure patterns thus declined.

Table 1.2 Owner occupation of housing with and without mortgages in Ireland, 1973 to 1999–2000

Per cent of total dwellings	1973	1981	1991	1999–2000
Owner occupied	69	74	79	82
With mortgage	22	34	41	35
Without mortgage	47	40	38	47

Source: 1973 Household Budget Survey; Census of Population 1981, 1991; Household Budget Survey 1999–2000

1.3 SOCIAL CHARACTERISTICS OF HOMEOWNERS

Given the primary focus in this study on home ownership, it is worth examining the current pattern of home ownership in more detail. For this purpose we rely here on data from the 2000 Living in Ireland (LII) Survey, which allows us to look at the characteristics of the households in the various tenures in some depth (this survey is described in detail in Layte *et al.* 2001 and Nolan *et al.* 2002). We saw earlier that the home ownership rate in Ireland is higher in rural than in urban areas, but how does it vary by other characteristics, such as the household's age, income and social class?

1.3.1 Owner Occupation and Age

We look first at the relationship between tenure and age. Table 1.3 shows how the extent of owner occupation varies with the age of the household head or 'reference person', that is, the person responsible for the rent or mortgage, or when a couple are jointly responsible, the older of the two. We see that owner occupation increases sharply as one moves from the under-35 to the 35–44 age range but then flattens out, with only a relatively modest further increase up to the 65–74 age range, after which it falls away.

The proportion of owner-occupied housing which is mortgage free (outright owner occupation) has a more pronounced and uniform age gradient, in keeping with rising incidence of mortgage clearing with rising age. Outright owner occupation is most prevalent among those where the reference person is aged over 64 but not over 74. It is worth noting that about one-quarter of this group have purchased their housing from the public authorities, whereas the corresponding figure is lower for those at both older and, more particularly, younger ages. This reflects the impact of a surge in sales of the public housing stock by the public authorities in the 1970s and 1980s (see Chapter 2).

Table 1.3 Housing tenure by age

Age of household reference person	Per cent owner occupier			Per cent acquired through tenant purchase from local authority*
	With mortgage	Without mortgage	All	
Under 35	47.0	6.2	53.2	8.2
35–44	65.5	16.5	83.0	11.2
45–54	48.1	39.0	87.1	17.1
55–64	24.7	60.3	86.0	20.8
65–74	11.7	80.8	92.5	26.0
75 and over	4.5	77.4	81.9	18.8

* Refers to present owner only; does not include dwellings purchased from local authority by previous owner.
Source: Living in Ireland Survey 2000

Thus, owner occupation is very high in Ireland throughout the age range, but the variation in its extent will have implications for the distribution of assets held in the form of housing, as discussed later on. Compared with patterns for other countries (as described by Lynch 2001), this gap between the proportion of older people who are owner occupiers compared to younger people who are owner occupiers in Ireland is similar to several other countries with high overall ownership rates, such as Spain, Italy and the US, though it is wider than in Canada.

1.3.2 Owner Occupation, Income and Social Class
One might expect the extent of owner occupation to vary not only by age but also by income. Table 1.4 shows that in Ireland there is an extremely high level of home ownership throughout the income distribution, categorising households in terms of total disposable household income (without any adjustment for differences in household size or composition). Towards the top of the income distribution the percentage in owner occupation approaches 90 per cent, but even for the bottom quintile it is as high as 60 per cent.

Table 1.4 Housing tenure by income

Income quintile	Per cent owner occupier
Bottom	59.5
2	78.9
3	84.3
4	87.6
Top	86.6

Source: Living in Ireland Survey 2000

Table 1.5 Housing tenure by social class

Social class	Per cent owner occupier
Higher service	95.0
Lower service	88.0
Higher routine non-manual	81.4
Lower routine non-manual	60.4
Self-employed with employees	84.8
Self-employed without employees	93.4
Technical/supervisory	91.1
Skilled manual	82.4
Semi-skilled manual	75.2
Unskilled manual	62.2
Agricultural workers	75.5
Farmers	97.1

Source: Living in Ireland Survey 2000

Perhaps even more strikingly, Table 1.5 shows the extent to which owner occupation is the dominant form of tenure across the social classes. Using the 12-category version of the Erikson-Goldthorpe social class schema, we see that towards the top of the class hierarchy about 95 per cent of the higher service class, the self-employed without employees and farmers are in owner occupation. However, even for the lower routine non-manual and unskilled manual classes, once again about 60 per cent are owner occupiers.

1.4 IRELAND'S HOUSING TENURE IN COMPARATIVE PERSPECTIVE

We can now place Irish patterns of home ownership in a comparative European context using data from the 1996 European Community Household Panel Survey (Watson 2003). Table 1.6 shows that in the mid-1990s Ireland and Spain had the highest rates of home ownership in the EU, at 80 to 81 per cent. However, if we look at levels of outright home ownership, that is, homes owned without mortgage debt, Ireland was closer to the centre of the EU range. The four southern European countries (Greece, Italy, Spain and Portugal) had higher rates of outright home ownership than Ireland, while Belgium and Finland had similar rates to Ireland's. The distribution of rates of outright home ownership across the EU indicate that at one extreme (represented by Greece and Italy) few homeowners have a mortgage, while at the other extreme (represented by the Netherlands and Denmark) the vast majority of homeowners have mortgages. These patterns are reflected in the differing levels of aggregate mortgage indebtedness relative to GDP across EU countries, also shown in Table 1.6. Mortgage indebtedness is low in the countries with high levels of outright home ownership and is highest in the countries where outright home ownership is rare.

Table 1.6 Tenure patterns in 14 EU countries (per cent), 1996

	Owner			Social renter	Private renter	Rent free	Mortgage debt as per cent of GDP in 2000
	All	With mortgage	Without mortgage				
Spain	80.8	18.8	62.1	0.8	12.0	6.4	18.5
Ireland	80.3	38.1	42.3	11.0	6.4	2.2	27.2
Greece	75.9	7.0	68.9	0.2	21.0	2.9	5.2
Italy	73.2	10.9	62.3	5.7	13.4	7.6	7.5
Belgium	73.2	32.2	40.9	7.0	17.3	2.5	21.5
Luxembourg	70.1	35.5	34.6	2.9	23.6	3.4	
UK	68.3	41.5	26.8	23.1	6.9	1.7	60.8
Portugal	66.3	14.4	51.9	3.7	20.1	9.9	22.2
Finland	64.5	27.4	37.2	17.0	16.2	2.3	31.1
France	53.3	24.4	29.0	16.8	24.1	5.8	20.4
Denmark	52.5	45.5	7.1	27.5	19.4	0.6	58.5
Austria	50.4	20.0	30.4	19.9	23.0	6.7	
Netherlands	49.0	41.7	7.3	42.1	7.8	1.1	54.2
Germany	40.2	18.6	21.6	12.5	43.2	4.1	48.5

Source: European Community Household Panel Survey 1996; Housing Statistics of the European Union 2001

Aside from differences in levels of home ownership, EU countries also differ in the mix of alternatives to ownership tenure that they offer to households. Ireland has a particularly small private rented sector by EU standards.[3] The Netherlands and the UK also have small private rented sectors, but their social rented sectors are large. In Germany the private rented sector is

---

3. The estimate of the size of Ireland's private rented sector produced by the European Community Household Panel Survey is on the low side, possibly reflecting sampling error. However, even the higher estimates produced by a range of national sources (see p. 3 above) still leave Ireland with a distinctively small private rented sector by EU standards.

large (43 per cent) while the social rented sector is small (12.5 per cent). Most countries with high levels of home ownership (such as the southern European countries, Belgium and Luxembourg) tend to rely on private rented accommodation as the main alternative to home ownership and to have small social rented sectors. In Ireland, the smallness of the private rented sector is anomalous in light of Ireland's large young-adult population. Since young people have a particular need for the flexible, easy-access accommodation that the private rented sector normally provides, one would expect the Irish housing system to respond with a substantial supply of housing in this sector. Yet a combination of factors has brought about the opposite situation, where the supply of private rented accommodation is distinctively small. The implications of this pattern are important to housing outcomes in Ireland and will be returned to below.

1.5 HOUSE PRICES

The recent rapid and sustained increase in house prices in Ireland has focused a great deal of attention on the housing market, and one of the key issues for this study is the implications of that surge in prices for poverty and wealth. However, it is important to first set this in historical context. As Figure 1.2 illustrates, data on house prices in Ireland since 1970 suggest that until the recent economic boom, the rate of increase in house prices largely kept pace with overall consumer prices. Real house prices rose somewhat in the late 1980s but then fell back slightly, and by the late 1980s were only marginally higher than they had been in 1970. After 1994, however, an unprecedented surge of economic growth, a sharp rise in disposable incomes (partly fuelled by income tax cuts), a fall in interest rates and substantial growth in the size of the young-adult population led to explosive growth in demand for housing. As a result, the average house price increased by 240 per cent in nominal terms and by 204 per cent in real terms between 1995 and 2000 (the nominal increase was from €76,000 to €180,000).

Figure 1.2 Trends in house prices in Ireland, 1970–2000 in current and constant (1996) prices (€)

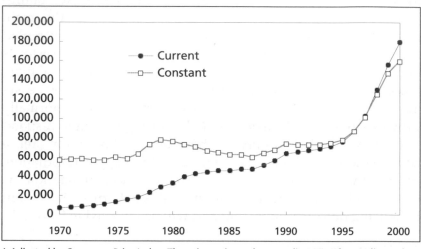

* Adjusted by Consumer Price Index. The price series makes no adjustment for quality and includes both new and second-hand house prices.

Source: Department of the Environment, Annual Bulletin of Housing Statistics

Housing assets are often thought of as an inflation beater in an Irish context, which can contribute to the demand for home purchase. The effects of inflation on house prices and the cost of capital for housing are complex (Irvine 1974), but direct effects of inflation are evident both in real interest rates and house price rises. Since 1965 interest rates for home purchasers in Ireland, when discounted for inflation, were either very low or negative from the late 1960s to the early 1980s and again in the late 1990s, as Figure 1.3 shows. Over the whole period from the mid-1960s, it was only from the mid-1980s to the mid-1990s that real interest rates exceeded 5 per cent. The impact of European monetary union on interest rates is evident in the late 1990s, as real interest rates fell more or less to zero despite the overheated state of the housing market in Ireland at that time.

Figure 1.3 Mortgage interest rates and inflation in Ireland, 1965–2001

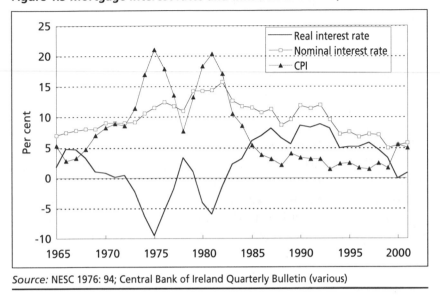

Source: NESC 1976: 94; Central Bank of Ireland Quarterly Bulletin (various)

The combination of high inflation and low real interest rates so often found in Ireland since the 1960s had a beneficial effect for home purchasers. It greatly reduced the real cost to house-holders of servicing mortgage debt and thus provided a major impetus to mortgage-financed home purchase. For example, for householders aged in their mid-40s in 1993–4, most of whom would have taken out their mortgages in the late 1970s, the cumulative inflationary impact in the early years of their mort-gage would have slashed the real value of their outstanding capital balances by as much as half (in the five-year period 1978–83 alone the cumulative Consumer Price Index increase was 108 per cent). In real terms, therefore, inflation would have done more to reduce the capital balance of mortgages than the householders' actual mortgage payments. As already men-tioned, since interest rates over the intervening period failed to rise sufficiently to compensate for inflation, the erosion of the value of mortgage repayment costs over time for householders was real, consistent and large. In the meantime, house prices more or less kept pace with inflation up to the early 1990s so that the real price of dwellings held up even as the real value of the debt on dwellings shrank.

The positive effects of inflation for mortgage borrowers represented an important distributive mechanism that has been little noted to date: the point-in-time hidden transfers from savers to borrowers implicit in the inflation-ridden credit markets that have frequently prevailed in Ireland since the 1960s. Through their willingness to place funds on deposit at rates of interest that were low or negative in real terms, savers enabled those funds to be made available to borrowers at correspondingly favourable terms. Thus, savers lost and borrowers gained at their expense. As we shall see below, the state (and thus the taxpayer) subsidised house purchase through various tax breaks and grants, but for many periods over recent decades savers did likewise, perhaps to a greater degree, through the liquidity made available for mortgage borrowers at low or even negative rates of interest.

1.6 'AFFORDABILITY'

Much of the recent debate about housing in Ireland has focused on the impact of the surge in house prices on the affordability of owner-occupied housing. Affordability is a complex and somewhat slippery concept, however, and it is necessary to be careful both in specifying what one is trying to measure and in how it is then captured using the available data. We examine this issue further in Chapter 3 in connection with household expenditures on mortgages and rents, but here we provide an initial outline of the issues based on aggregate house price and household income data.

The main concern that has been articulated about rising house prices is that many potential homebuyers are being priced out of the market – they cannot afford to buy because prices have surged ahead of incomes. Available indicators of trends in the affordability of housing over time then take a number of forms. The most obvious is to simply relate trends in average house prices to those in average earnings. This would indeed show a widening gap emerging in Ireland since the mid-1990s (for example, see Downey 1998: 76, Chart 5.1).

However, it is particularly important in the Irish case that income after tax rather than simply average earnings be employed, given the scale of the cuts in personal taxation over the second half of the 1990s. This complicates the construction of affordability indices, since the readily available statistical series on earnings – notably the average industrial earnings series produced by the Central Statistics Office (CSO) every quarter – relate to earnings before deduction of income tax and social insurance contributions. Since the amount deducted in tax from someone on, say, average industrial earnings will depend on their other circumstances – notably marital status and earnings of their spouse, if any – assumptions have to be made to arrive at a post-tax figure. A common approach is to take specified illustrative cases – for example, a married couple with one earner on the average industrial wage or a particular multiple of it, or two earners, one on the average industrial wage and one on the average wage for non-industrial workers.

An alternative is to take the only post-tax aggregate income series regularly produced by the CSO, the Personal Disposable Income aggregate in the National Accounts, as the income measure and divide it by the number of households in each year. This has the advantage that it also reflects incomes other than employee earnings or the even narrower earnings for employees in industry only. Even with this broader, post-tax income measure, Figure 1.4 shows that house prices have risen much more rapidly than personal disposable income on average since 1995–6. (The gap is particularly pronounced if one only looks at houses in the Dublin area, though this does not take into account that income may have also increased more rapidly there.) The average new house is now four times annual disposable household income, compared to a multiple of less than three in 1996.

Figure 1.4 New house prices as a multiple of average disposable income, 1976–2000

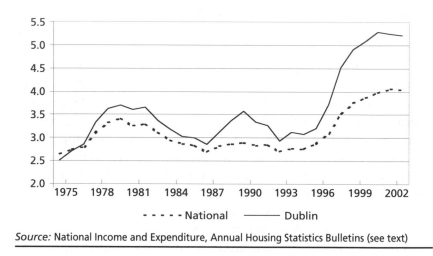

Source: National Income and Expenditure, Annual Housing Statistics Bulletins (see text)

Comparing prices with earnings or incomes still misses a critically important part of the story, since the cost of servicing debt taken on for house purchase varies as interest rates fluctuate. Some affordability measures thus relate trends in the cost of servicing a typical mortgage required to buy a new home for a first-time buyer at the average price to trends in average disposable incomes. It is striking to note that despite the price explosion in the period 1995–2000, aggregate measures of affordability constructed in this way for Ireland show only moderate worsening during the 1990s (Downey 1998; Bacon and Associates 1998). By 2000 and 2001, at the peak of the house price rise, the combination of falling interest rates and rising after-tax incomes meant that the repayment burden was somewhat worse than in the mid-1990s but was still reasonably low by historical standards. As an example, Figure 1.5 shows mortgage repayments for someone borrowing 90 per cent of the average new house price over a 20-year term and paying the current mortgage interest rate in each year (the estimates of household disposable income used here are drawn from

National Accounts data). Their repayments as a percentage of household disposable income rose from a point below 24 per cent in 1996 to an estimated 28 per cent in 2003. However, this compares favourably to corresponding levels in excess of 30 per cent in 1989–91 and in excess of 45 per cent in the late 1970s and early 1980s. Thus, according to these admittedly crude aggregate estimates, house purchase is a good deal more affordable now than it has been at various points in the recent past (for further exploration of this issue based on household micro-data, see Chapter 5).

Figure 1.5 Repayments as a proportion of disposable income

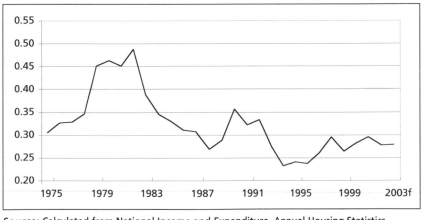

Source: Calculated from National Income and Expenditure, Annual Housing Statistics Bulletins (see text)

Two points should be made about these affordability measures. The first is that the repayment burden is highly sensitive to the interest rate. Each one-point increase in the interest rate would add over two points to the repayments as a percentage of disposable income. Homeowners who are not particularly stretched to meet mortgage repayments at current interest rates could therefore find themselves much more heavily burdened if interest rates were to rise significantly from their current low levels, or if their incomes were to fall as a result of factors such as unemployment.

The second point is that these measures capture the repayment burden for those who have succeeded in purchasing a house. Analysis of household micro-data in subsequent chapters supports the notion that the mortgage repayment burden is not in fact very high for many Irish households, even in the early stages of family formation and house purchase. However, the other crucial element in the capacity to buy a house is raising the deposit required, even if a mortgage lender advances 90 per cent of the purchase price. The difficulty posed by down-payment requirements has always been present in the house purchase system, and it is not clear that the obstacle it poses is any greater now than it was in the past. It is interesting to note that a substantial proportion of new house purchasers appear to need to borrow considerably less than the 90 per cent (or more) of the purchase price now made available by mortgage lenders. Data supplied to the Economic and Social Research Institute by one major lending agency suggests that the average loan-to-value ratio of first-time mortgage borrowers is as low as 72 per cent. Where the remainder of the purchase price is coming from is not clear – prior savings, inheritances, contributions from parents and other family members could all play a role.

The real affordability 'crunch' in terms of house purchase may arise for someone living in private rented housing and facing rapidly rising rents while trying to accumulate an ever-growing deposit and without such contributions from extended family to allow them to access the house purchase market. This possibility focuses attention on costs and affordability in the private rented sector, which receives less notice than house purchase but where affordability may indeed be an extremely important issue for many households there – a theme to which we return later in this study.

Chapter 2

HOME OWNERSHIP AND PUBLIC POLICY IN IRELAND

2.1 INTRODUCTION

The high level of home ownership in Ireland is not simply an accident. Public policy has played a central role over a long period in promoting owner occupation, and in the past, certain aspects of that role have been the dominant influence. We have seen in the previous chapter that low real interest rates and high inflation – factors which themselves have been influenced by public policy – have often acted in favour of house purchasers, mainly by sharply reducing the real cost of mortgage credit to borrowers.

In this chapter we consider aspects of public policy that were more directly targeted on the housing system itself rather than on the environment in which the housing system operated, and focus in particular on those geared to the promotion of home ownership. Housing policy in general has changed a great deal in recent years and the nature and direction of its effects on the growth of home ownership has also changed. Some aspects of that change have already been referred to, most notably the smaller role for social housing which has arisen from the fiscal cutbacks of the late 1980s (see Chapter 1 above). We now outline some additional aspects of the state's influence on housing tenure patterns, looking first at the historical origins and development of that influence and then concentrating on recent developments.

2.2 LAND REFORM AND SOCIAL HOUSING

A number of strands of public policy were central to what was in effect a revolution over the course of the twentieth century that changed Irish households from being predominantly renters at the beginning of the century to predominantly homeowners at the end. The first was the rural land reform carried out from the 1890s to the 1920s. Based on purchase arrangements that because of generous state subsidies were favourable to both landlords and tenants, this reform transferred ownership of some 85 per cent of the agricultural land of Ireland, and the dwelling stock which went with it, from around 19,000 proprietors in the early 1880s to approximately 400,000 smallholders (Fahey 2002). (The precise number of landlords and smallholders involved varies according to the year in which they are counted, as the numbers of both were in steady decline over the period.) Consequently, owner occupation was already the dominant tenure in rural Ireland by the time of the Second World War.

The second strand of public policy that promoted owner occupation was a direct outgrowth of the first. It took the form of the early development of a rural social authority housing programme provided by local authorities, which eventually converted into an alternative and heavily subsidised route to home ownership for working-class households in urban as well as rural areas. This programme crystallised in the first decade of the twentieth century as a means to placate agricultural labourers for their exclusion from the largesse granted to tenant farmers under the land reform programme. Every major step forward in land reform legislation in this period was paralleled by the provision of generously subsidised local authority rental housing for rural labourers, the category of whom eventually extended to encompass the entire working class outside of the major towns and cities. By the First World War, this programme had endowed the rural working class with high-quality, low-cost social housing and also created a social housing sector that was precociously large for its time (Fraser 1996).

Echoing the precedents set by land reform, rural social housing soon evolved in the direction of home ownership. A generously subsidised tenant purchase scheme for rural social housing was introduced in the 1936 Labourers Act, with purchase annuities initially set at 75 per cent of pre-purchase rents. In the early 1950s purchase annuities were reduced to 50 per cent of rents, echoing the give-away terms then enjoyed by farmers. (The 1933 Land Act had reduced the already low purchase annuities payable by farmers under earlier land acts by half – see Walsh 1999.) Predictable consequences followed: by 1964, 80 per cent of the housing built under the rural social housing programme had been transferred to the ownership of sitting tenants (Minister for Local Government 1964).

The combined precedents set by rural land reform and rural social housing percolated in the 1960s and 1970s into urban social housing, which had been massively expanded in the slum clearance programmes of the 1930s and 1940s. The 1966 Housing Act, adopting and updating the model established for rural social housing in the 1930s, provided for simplified schemes of tenant purchase of local authority housing in urban as well as rural areas. These schemes were widely implemented from the early 1970s onwards, resulting in waves of heavy selling of urban local authority housing. Though the local authority house building programme ran to high levels from the late 1960s to the 1980s, older public housing was sold as fast as new public housing was built, with the result that the public housing stock remained static in absolute size (at around 100,000 dwellings) and shrank as a share of the total housing stock (from 18.4 per cent in 1961 to 9.7 per cent in 1991 – see Table 1.1 above). Purchase prices for local authority housing were typically extremely favourable to tenants. The tenant purchase scheme implemented by Dublin Corporation in the late 1980s, for example, entailed discounts on the market value of housing of up to 60 per cent (Lord Mayor's Commission on Housing 1993).

The consequence for Irish social housing was that by the early 1990s, of the 330,000 dwellings built by local authorities over the previous century, some 220,000 had been sold to tenants (O'Connell and Fahey 1999: 38), which amounted to one in four of the homes in private ownership in Ireland by that time. They were thus a major contributor to the overall tenure revolution

and in particular were the dominant means of access to home ownership for the urban and rural working classes.

2.3 SUBSIDISING HOUSE BUILDING AND HOME OWNERSHIP

In addition to land reform and the sale of local authority housing to tenants, the third strand of state support for home ownership took the form of a shifting body of grants and tax breaks for privately built owner-occupied housing. Grants for private house building were first introduced in the 1920s and have remained a permanent feature of housing policy since then. By the 1950s, the scale of private housing grants combined with social housing expenditure was such that, according to estimates by the UN's Economic Commission for Europe, 75 per cent of capital for housing construction originated from the state, compared to a norm of 50 per cent in Europe (quoted in Ó hUigínn 1959–60: 49). In the early 1960s, it was estimated that 98 per cent of the housing stock built in the previous 15 years had received some form of public subsidy (Pfretzschner 1965: 37). In the late 1970s, a further 'period of very aggressive support for owner occupation was commenced', with the abolition of virtually all tax on owner-occupied housing and the retention of mortgage interest relief (McCashin 2000). In 1987, it was estimated that of a total of £552 million provided in public subsidies to housing, £218 million (39 per cent) went to owner occupiers and of that, £175 million (or 80 per cent) was accounted for by tax reliefs on expenditure related to house purchase (NESC 1988: 60).

The principal forms of such tax subsidy are widely known in other countries: the non-taxation of imputed income arising from home ownership, income tax relief for mortgage interest payments and the non-taxation of capital gains arising in connection with principal private residences (Joumard 2001). Imputed income arising from owner occupation was charged to tax on a notional basis in Ireland during the early decades of income taxation. However, as in other countries with similar tax provisions, the valuations of imputed income were generally low, yielded little tax revenue and had little impact on house purchase behaviour (the tax yield from this source in 1961 was estimated at £325,000, which was about 1 per cent of total income tax – Kaim-Caudle 1965; Commission on Taxation 1982: 133–4; NESC 1976: 40). The practice was abolished in 1969 and has not been reinstated since. The burden of taxation on residential property was further lightened in 1978 when domestic dwellings were exempted from rates.

Income tax relief on mortgage interest for home purchase was allowed in full and at marginal tax rates until 1974. The amount of interest allowable was then capped (albeit at a high level) and its significance as a subsidy remained large until the late 1980s.[1] Since then, however, its significance has sharply declined, partly because inflation has eroded the value of amounts of interest allowable against tax and partly because tax rates have fallen. Furthermore, during the mid-1980s tax relief on mortgage interest was reduced from the marginal to the standard rate, which is now at 20 per cent. As a result of these developments, mortgage interest relief at present plays a much smaller role in housing finance than it did up to the mid-1980s. In 1987 it was worth the equivalent of 6.5 per cent of income tax receipts (£175 million), compared to 0.2 per cent in 1999–2000 (€158 million).

Capital gains arising from the sale of a principal private residence are entirely exempt from tax. The precise importance of this aspect of housing taxation is difficult to estimate since it is greatly influenced by how capital gains are quantified (depending, for example, on whether and how allowances are made for inflation, interest payments and depreciation) and the rate at which they are taxed. The rate of capital gains tax was reduced from 40 per cent to 20 per cent in Ireland in 1997, thus halving the implicit tax benefit arising from non-taxation of capital gains in owner-occupied housing.

---

1. Tax reliefs were also allowed for life insurance premiums until the late 1980s. This encouraged the growth of endowment mortgages where life insurance contributions were used as the means to amortise the debt. For a brief overview of the complex history of these reliefs, see Commission on Taxation (1982: 173–6).

Though owner-occupied dwellings are lightly taxed in most ways, they are subject to one significant form of taxation – stamp duty on housing transactions, payable by the purchaser. Current rates of stamp duty range from zero for properties worth less than €127,000 to 9 per cent for properties worth over €635,000. The majority of house sales attract stamp duty at the medium rates of either 4 or 5 per cent (in 2002, the average house price in Ireland was €180,000 – see below). To aid first-time house buyers, they receive special treatment – they are exempt from stamp duty for lower-cost housing and receive a 25 per cent discount on stamp duty for medium-cost housing. Taken in conjunction with sales costs and legal fees, stamp duty amounts to a significant element of overall house purchase costs. The tax take from stamp duty on land and property (excluding stocks and shares) increased almost four-fold between 1994 and 2000 (from €181 million to €674 million). The data published by the Revenue Commissioners does not distinguish the share of this tax take accounted for housing, so it is not possible to assess the tax burden on housing that stamp duty now represents.

2.4 THE STATE AND MORTGAGE LENDING

A final direct support for house purchase provided by the state was the large role played by local authority mortgage lending up to 1987. Under the Small Dwellings Acquisitions Acts, the first of which dates from 1899, local authorities were empowered to provide mortgage financing for private housing, with no restriction on their clientele up to 1955 but with an increasing focus on the less well-off after that date. Prior to economic take-off in the 1960s, local authorities were often the primary source of mortgage financing. While the scale of local authority mortgage lending fluctuated during the 1970s, loans from this source accounted for over one-third of all new mortgages by value (Figure 2.1) and for nearly half of all new mortgage loans by number in this period.[2] During the mid-1980s, local authority

---

2. The Housing Finance Agency was set up by statute in 1981 to borrow and advance funds to local authorities for this and other housing activities.

mortgages accounted for over 25 per cent of new loans by value. Fiscal retrenchment in 1987 sharply reduced the funds available to local authorities for lending purposes, and by the early 1990s their share of the mortgage market had dwindled to below 2 per cent of the total. Such lending now plays little role in financing house purchase, thus potential purchasers are perforce reliant on the private mortgage market.

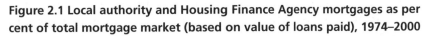

Figure 2.1 Local authority and Housing Finance Agency mortgages as per cent of total mortgage market (based on value of loans paid), 1974–2000

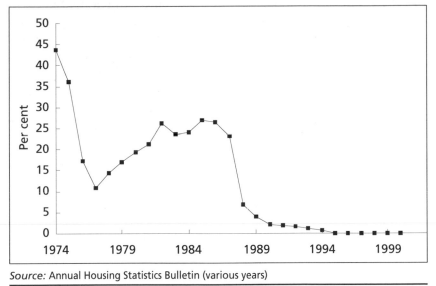

Source: Annual Housing Statistics Bulletin (various years)

While the interest rates on local authority loans were at best only marginally more attractive than commercial rates, they offered higher loan to value ratios than commercial lenders (usually up to 95 per cent). They also took a more flexible approach to issues such as eligibility criteria for loans, repayment schedules and repayment terms. As such, they provided an important additional resource for home ownership among less well-off households, over and above that provided by the sale of local authority housing.

In addition to its role in providing credit to less well-off households, local authority mortgage lending had a broader significance as a major additional source of finance for private house building in periods when private sector credit became scarce. Prior to the advent of European monetary union in the 1990s, funds for lending in the private sector sometimes fell below demand on account of low real interest rates and a consequent fall-off in deposits. As a result, private mortgage credit was periodically subject to rationing, a pattern that particularly occurred during the era of low real interest rates in the 1970s and early 1980s. Public sector mortgages helped meet the credit shortfall which resulted. Those mortgages were funded by government borrowing rather than domestic savings and provided a means of accessing international capital markets where exchange rate risk was not passed on to the borrower, thereby escaping the constraints imposed by levels of savings in the Irish economy and the barriers to international borrowing by the private sector imposed by exchange rate risk. They ensured a flow of funds for Irish mortgage borrowers which would not otherwise have been available and which expanded access to mortgage credit beyond what would have been possible in a wholly private mortgage system. That additional supply of funds goes a long way to explaining how a reasonably adequate flow of mortgage credit could be sustained, even when real interest rates were well below the level needed to make building society savings attractive to depositors.

In the aftermath of European monetary union in the 1990s, interest rates in Ireland and the amounts of capital available for lending have been determined by broader European patterns and thus have become detached from supply and demand factors in the domestic financial market. The abundance and low cost of private credit now matches what was formerly available through public sector mortgages and so the need for public mortgages has greatly declined. However, in considering the increased demand and broader clientele for private sector mortgages that emerged in the 1990s, it must be kept in mind that that clientele now encompasses the types of households which formerly would have been catered for by local authority mortgage lending and which therefore, in a certain sense, came under the umbrella of public sector housing provision, at least as far as financing is concerned. Thus, private sector mortgages serve a wider segment of the population than they did in the past.

2.5 CONCLUSION

This chapter has shown that the history of state intervention in the housing system in Ireland is long and deep and has played a major role in the growth of home ownership over the past hundred years. Land reform in the early part of the twentieth century and tenant purchase of local authority housing, which originated in the 1930s and reached especially high levels in the 1970s and 1980s, were two especially important elements in that role. A wide range of grants, tax breaks and mortgage services for the provision of privately built housing has also been available. The precise contribution of these measures to the growth of owner occupation is uncertain. Their relative importance in comparison to other factors that supported home ownership, such as the long periods of low real interest rates and high inflation referred to in Chapter 1, is difficult to evaluate.

Looking at developments in recent years, it is evident that state supports for owner occupation have declined in a number of important respects, primarily as a legacy of the fiscal cutbacks of the late 1980s. Tenant purchase of local authority rental dwellings has become relatively unimportant, partly because the local authority sector is now too small to provide a large reservoir of housing for sale and partly because tenants who would have the resources to buy are no longer found in large numbers in the local authority rented sector. The state's formerly large role in mortgage lending (in the form of mortgage provision by local authorities and the Housing Finance Agency) has also all but disappeared since 1987, so that low-income house purchasers must now rely on private rather than public mortgage credit. Grants and tax breaks for home purchase have also become less extensive, particularly since restrictions on mortgage interest relief mean that its real value to home purchasers is now only a fraction of what it was at its peak in the years prior to 1987. At the same time, stamp duty impositions have increased and have become a substantial burden on house purchasers, especially those buying more expensive properties. Some privileging of owner occupation remains in place, such as exemption from capital gains tax and non-taxation of imputed rental income, but the overall effect of recent developments has been to scale back the state's previously strong role in promoting home ownership.

This scaling back has not been sufficient to hold down house prices or restrain demand for new housing construction, though had it not been pursued the housing market might have heated up even more than it did. However, it has taken place in the context of changing state provision for both social and private rented housing. The interaction between these developments has had a range of effects, which we will return to later in our overall assessment of recent trends in the housing market.

Chapter 3

HOUSEHOLD EXPENDITURE ON HOUSING IN IRELAND

3.1 INTRODUCTION

The pattern of housing tenure clearly has important conse-quences for household expenditure on housing. Someone who owns their home outright avoids rent and mortgage payments and thus has more money available for non-housing consump-tion than someone on the same income facing rent or mortgage payments. Of course, owner occupiers are not automatically better off than renters, even if they are spending less on housing. Even the outright homeowner spending nothing on rent or mortgage could be losing out if the capital invested in the house would have yielded a higher rate of return in other forms of investment sufficient to cover the cost of renting and leave a surplus available for higher consumption. Thus, the precise balance of advantage between the different tenure categories varies enormously, depending on both current and historical conditions concerning house prices, mortgage interest rates, inflation, housing subsidies and rates of return to alternative uses of capital.

In place of the complex analysis that a full account of these patterns would entail, we adopt a simpler approach here, concentrating on direct, proximate links between housing tenure and household expenditure on housing. We look in detail at how expenditure on housing has evolved over time in Ireland for those in different tenures and at its variation across and within tenures in the most recent data. We then look at how many households might be revealed by conventional measurement approaches to face an 'affordability' problem in terms of the level of housing expenditure relative to their income.

3.2 Household Expenditure on Housing over Time in Ireland

We first examine trends over time in the spending on housing associated with the different housing tenures, focusing on the period covered by national Household Budget Surveys, that is, from 1973 to 1999–2000. Table 3.1 sets out the full data on which our discussion will be based and some graphs based on that table will help to highlight the key trends.

Figure 3.1 places changing levels of rent and mortgage payments for Irish households since 1973 in context by outlining the growth in households' total current financial resources, distinguishing homeowners without a mortgage, homeowners with a mortgage, those renting in the private sector and those renting social housing. Total household expenditure (expressed in constant euros at 2000 prices) is the indicator of financial resources used at this point. (Expenditure is usually regarded as less liable to under-reporting in survey data than income and so is used here as a measure of household financial resources when it is available in the data.) The graph shows that all four groups had a marked increase in average household expenditure in real terms during the 1970s. A slight decline set in during the 1980s, followed by a strong and sustained recovery after 1987. The overall effect was that, in general, real household expenditure grew substantially over the period 1973 to 1999–2000.

However, the extent of growth of total household expenditure differed sharply across the four tenure categories, ranging from a 115 per cent increase among private renters to a 6 per cent increase among social renters. Consequently, the gaps in average household expenditure across the groups widened dramatically. In 1973, for example, total household expenditure for the average owner with a mortgage was 1.4 times that of social renters, but by 1999–2000 this multiple was 2.5 times. Private renters experienced the largest increase in total household expenditure, thus indicating large increases in incomes in that sector. In 1973 their average household expenditure was the lowest of all the tenure categories, marginally below that of social renters, yet by 1999–2000 it had risen to almost double that

Table 3.1 Trends in housing expenditure indicators by tenure, Ireland, 1973–2000

	1973	1980	1987	1994–5	1999–2000	Per cent change 1973–2000
Outright owner						
Mortgage payments (€)	0.00	0.00	0.00	0.00	0.00	0
Other housing expenditure (€)	14.93	9.77	14.13	12.31	14.30	-4
Total household expenditure (€)	339.61	379.89	352.87	378.77	480.41	41
Mortgage as per cent of total	0.00	0.00	0.00	0.00	0.00	0
Other as per cent of total	4.40	2.57	4.00	3.25	2.98	-32
Persons per household (no.)	3.71	3.42	3.07	2.86	2.68	-28
Total equivalised household expenditure (€)	176.32	205.42	201.39	223.97	293.46	66
Owner with mortgage						
Mortgage payments (€)	28.71	45.44	51.78	65.19	73.79	157
Other housing expenditure (€)	23.56	15.79	13.00	16.85	22.37	-5
Total household expenditure (€)	404.10	577.12	526.59	625.89	767.40	90
Mortgage as per cent of total	7.10	7.90	9.80	10.40	9.60	35
Other as per cent of total	5.83	2.74	2.47	2.69	2.92	-50
Persons per household (no.)	4.56	4.41	4.15	3.95	3.76	-18
Total equivalised household expenditure (€)	189.24	274.82	258.49	314.92	395.76	109
Social renters						
Rent (€)	21.55	15.31	14.63	19.10	22.69	5
Other housing expenditure (€)	3.09	2.17	2.41	2.58	3.04	-2
Total household expenditure (€)	289.31	326.72	252.06	252.63	306.99	6
Rent as per cent of total	7.40	4.70	5.80	7.60	7.40	0
Other as per cent of total	1.10	0.70	1.00	1.00	1.00	-9
Persons per household (no.)	4.89	4.36	3.89	3.44	3.15	-36
Total equivalised household expenditure (€)	130.83	156.47	127.80	136.21	172.97	32
Private renters						
Rent (€)	35.14	39.48	45.25	80.26	126.30	259
Other housing expenditure (€)	2.75	5.87	6.21	1.53	4.97	81
Total household expenditure (€)	280.54	372.00	360.98	423.72	601.93	115
Rent as per cent of total	12.50	10.60	12.50	18.90	21.00	68
Other as per cent of total	1.00	1.60	1.70	0.40	0.80	-20
Persons per household (no.)	3.02	2.40	2.45	2.45	2.66	-12
Total equivalised household expenditure (€)	161.43	240.12	230.62	270.70	369.07	129

Note: Prices are expressed in constant 2000 terms (Consumer Price Index deflator). 'Other housing expenditure' consists of local authority charges, house insurance, repairs and decorations. Domestic rates are included in 'other housing expenditure' for owners (with and without mortgages) in 1973. Rates were abolished in 1977 and do not figure in the subsequent data. Total equivalised household expenditure is total household expenditure divided by the square root of the number of persons per household.

Source: Household Budget Surveys 1973, 1980, 1987, 1994–5, 1999–2000

of social renters and was also substantially higher than that of outright owners.

Figure 3.1 Total weekly household expenditure by housing tenure, 1973–2000

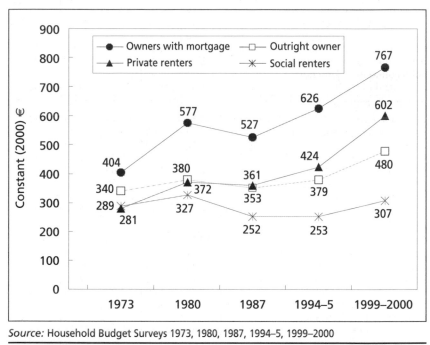

Source: Household Budget Surveys 1973, 1980, 1987, 1994–5, 1999–2000

Total household expenditure tells only part of the story since it does not take account of changes in household size. As household size generally tended to decline over this period, increases in individual consumption were even greater than gross household expenditure trends would suggest. In addition, as is shown by the data on number of persons per household in each tenure category in Table 3.1, decline in household size was unevenly spread across the tenures: the decline was largest among social renters and smallest among private renters. In fact, household size increased among private renters during the 1980s and 1990s, the only tenure category where this was so (this pattern may have reflected an increase in house sharing among private tenants as a way of coping with higher rents). If one adjusts household expenditure to take account of household size (to arrive at 'equivalised' household expenditure), somewhat different comparative rates of increase in expenditure emerge across tenures, as illustrated in Figure 3.2. (The adjustment for household size used here divides total household expenditure by the square root of the number of persons in the household, a widely used method of adjustment where detailed data on the age composition of households is not available).

Figure 3.2 Total weekly equivalised household expenditure by housing tenure, 1973–2000

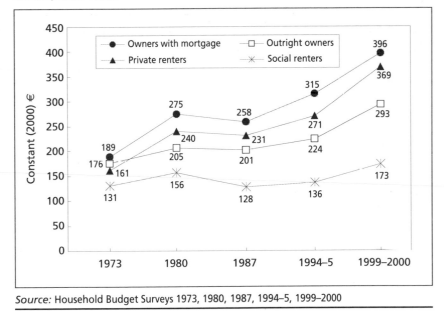

Source: Household Budget Surveys 1973, 1980, 1987, 1994–5, 1999–2000

We see that the relative position of social renters is most affected by this adjustment, as they had the largest decline (36 per cent) in household size over the period. Where they show an increase of only 6 per cent in average household expenditure before equivalisation over the period 1973–2000, they show a 32

33

per cent increase when equivalisation is taken into account. Private renters register an increase of 129 per cent in equivalised household expenditure compared to a non-equivalised increase of 115 per cent. Viewed in these terms, the widening of the gaps in equivalised household expenditure between tenure categories is still present and is quite strong, but is somewhat less extreme than for expenditure without any adjustment for household size.

We now come to trends in expenditure on rent and mortgage over time. Since outright owners have no such expenditure, the comparison across tenures is reduced to three categories – owners with a mortgage and private and social renters. Figure 3.3 shows the trend in absolute real mortgage/rent expenditure for these three categories since 1973.

Figure 3.3 Weekly rent/mortgage payments by housing tenure, 1973–2000

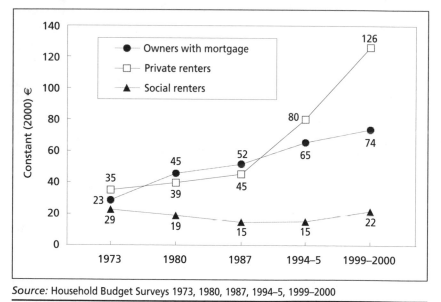

Source: Household Budget Surveys 1973, 1980, 1987, 1994–5, 1999–2000

The most striking change over the period occurred among private renters. Their average spending on rent increased only slightly between 1973 and 1987 but thereafter rose sharply. By 1999–2000, private rents, at an average of €126 per week, were 2.8 times greater in constant money terms than they had been in 1987, when they had averaged €45 per week.

It is notable here that this rapid increase was well underway in advance of the housing shortage and house price boom that occurred from 1994 onwards. However, it did coincide with the expansion of the SWA rent allowance scheme and the fall-off in the provision of new local authority housing referred to earlier. These developments meant that a significant portion of the demand for housing among the less well-off was transferred from the social housing sector to the private rental market from 1989 onwards (Fahey and Watson 1995: 166–84). SWA rent allowances for private rental accommodation became a func-tional alternative to differential rents in the local authority sector in the early 1990s, and the former perforce expanded to relieve the pressure caused by contraction in the supply of local authority accommodation after fiscal contraction in 1987. This transfer of demand for subsidised rental accommodation to the private sector is likely to have contributed to the rises in private rents, though its precise contribution is difficult to estimate. Aggregating up from Household Budget Survey data, we can estimate that the total annual rent bill for private tenants in 1999 was of the order of €719 million. Annual public expenditure on rent allowances in 1999 was just under €130 million (£100.5 million), which was about 18 per cent of the total rent bill. Thus, had rent allowances been entirely absent, the total available to tenants to pay private rents would have declined by about one-fifth (and possibly by less if tenants were able to provide replacement funds from other sources, including their own resources). Consequently, it would seem that rent allowances represented a significant but still far from dominant share of the total private rent bill. It thus can be considered as no more than one of a number of contributors to the rise in private rents during the 1990s.

Figure 3.3 shows that owners with a mortgage also registered an increase in expenditure, in this case in connection with mortgage payments, but the increase was smaller and more evenly spread over time than was the case for private renters. It is also notable that the upward trend was not intensified by the boom in house prices after 1994–5. In fact, the increase between 1994–5 and 1999–2000 (at €9 per week, or 13.8 per cent) was less than it was in the period between 1987 and 1994–5 (when it was €13 per week, or 25 per cent). Among social renters, no real increase in average spending on rent occurred – average social housing rents were about the same in real terms in 1999–2000 as they had been in 1973, and in fact had fallen considerably below those levels in the intervening decades.

Figure 3.4 shows the trend in rent/mortgage payments as a percentage of total household expenditure for the different groups. Here again the most striking changes are seen to have occurred among private renters. The share of their total household expenditure going on rent fell between 1973 and 1980 and rose back to the levels of 1973 by 1987. It then increased rapidly, rising from 12.5 per cent of household expenditure in 1987 to 18.9 per cent in 1994–5 and then to 21 per cent by 1999–2000. Among owners with a mortgage, Figure 3.4 shows that the share of household expenditure absorbed by mortgage payments rose during the 1970s and 1980s. However, echoing the disjunction with house price trends noted above, this share peaked at 10.4 per cent in 1994–5 and thereafter fell slightly to 9.6 per cent by 1999–2000.

Figure 3.4 Weekly rent/mortgage payments as percentage of total housing expenditure, 1973–2000

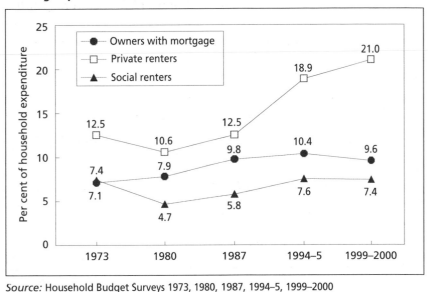

Source: Household Budget Surveys 1973, 1980, 1987, 1994–5, 1999–2000

It is worth comparing the shape of this trend in mortgage repayments with trends in the dominant influences on mortgage payment levels over the period, namely interest rates (shown in Figure 3.5) and trends in house price increases (already displayed in Chapter 2 and repeated here for convenience in Figure 3.6). This comparison suggests that the trend for mortgage payments as a proportion of total expenditure over time is closer in shape to that for real interest rates than for house price rises. In particular, the peaking in mortgage payments as a percentage of household expenditure in 1994–5, as shown in Figure 3.4, coincided with a peak in real interest rates at that time, as shown in Figure 3.5, while its subsequent slight fall-off followed a fall in interest rates and ran directly counter to the boom in house prices. These overall trends and influences on mortgage payments undoubtedly mask sharply different experiences for different categories of mortgage holders, particularly between new entrants to the housing market and those with older mortgages. Nevertheless, the relatively slight impact of recent house price rises on overall weekly mortgage expenditure as a proportion of income across all those with mortgages is striking.

Figure 3.5 Mortgage interest rates and inflation (Consumer Price Index) in Ireland, 1965–2001

Annual average of monthly mortgage interest rates

Source: NESC 1976: 94; Central Bank of Ireland Quarterly Bulletin (various)

Figure 3.4 shows that for social renters the share of household expenditure accounted for by rent declined sharply during the 1970s, falling below 5 per cent in 1980. Afterwards, it rose slowly to peak at 7.6 per cent in 1994–5 and was still at about that level in 1999–2000. This meant that the share of household expenditure going on rent among social renters was the same in 1999–2000 as it had been in 1973.

It is also worth briefly noting how other housing expenditure as recorded in the Household Budget Surveys and shown in Table 3.1 above has changed over this period. This currently consists mainly of house insurance, repairs and maintenance and accounts for just under 3 per cent of total household expenditure among homeowners (whether with or without a mortgage) and under 1 per cent among social and private renters. These percentages have remained relatively stable since 1981. However, for homeowners this expenditure fell substantially between 1973 and 1981 due to the abolition of domestic rates in 1978, which eliminated the main form of taxation on residential property which existed at that time. Though a residential property tax was introduced in the 1980s, it was levied on a much smaller proportion of households than had previously been subject to domestic rates and in any event was abolished after much controversy. Thus, after 1977 taxation of residential property is notable for its absence from housing-related expenditure for Irish households.

Figure 3.6 Trends in house prices in Ireland, 1970–2000

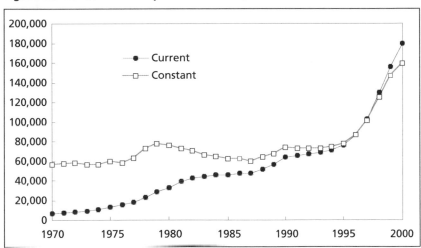

* Adjusted by Consumer Price Index. The price series makes no adjustment for quality and includes both new and second-hand house prices.
Source: Department of the Environment, Annual Bulletin of Housing Statistics

3.3 HOUSING EXPENDITURE AND THE LIFE CYCLE

It is useful to look in detail at how expenditure on housing varies across the life cycle, especially in view of recent concerns that housing cost rises in the latter half of the 1990s might have caused housing expenditures to bear down particularly on those in the early stages of family formation (for a more detailed analysis of this issue see Fahey 2003). The classification into family cycle stages employed by the CSO in the Household Budget Surveys distinguishes a 10-category grouping of households from 'young single' through to 'retired', which is useful for this purpose.

Figure 3.7 shows the way mortgage and rent as a share of total household expenditure varied across stages of the family cycle in both 1994–5 and 1999–2000. For those in the early stages of family formation, who are likely to include many new entrants

Figure 3.7 Rent/mortgage expenditure as per cent of total household expenditure by family cycle stage, 1994–5 and 1999–2000

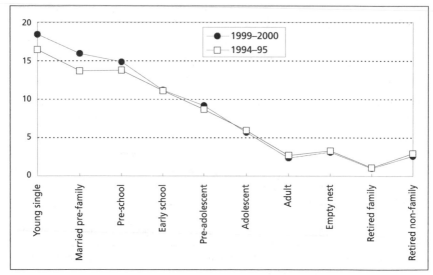

Note: Family cycle definitions: *Young single* – household head aged under 45, no children; *Married pre-family* – couple, wife aged under 45, no children; *Pre-school* – head with eldest resident child (ERC) aged 0–4 years; *Early school* – head with ERC aged 5–9 years; *Pre-adolescent* – head with ERC aged 10–14; *Adolescent* – head with ERC aged 15–19 years; *Adult* – head with ERC aged 20 years plus; *Empty nest* – couple, wife aged 45–64, no resident children; *Retired family* – couple, wife aged 65 years plus, no resident children; *Retired non-family* – head aged 65 years plus, no resident spouse or children.

Source: Household Budget Survey micro-data 1994–5 and 1999–2000

to the housing market, expenditure on mortgages increased as a share of total expenditure between the two time points and was a good deal higher than for those in the middle and later stages of the family cycle. However, in view of the rapid rise in house prices over the period in question, the increase in housing expenditures for those in the early family stages was modest and still left those expenditures at relatively low levels in 1999–2000 (at 18.4 per cent of total expenditure in the case of young single households and 15.9 per cent in the case of married pre-family households). For the other family cycle stages, the level of expenditure on mortgages was remarkably similar in the two time periods and declined to low levels as the family cycle progressed. By the time families reach the adolescent child stage, i.e. when the oldest child was aged 15–19 years and householders on average were aged in their mid-40s, rent and mortgage expenditures had fallen to around 7 per cent of household expenditure.

3.4 HOUSING EXPENDITURE AND 'AFFORDABILITY'

We return now to look in more detail at the question of the 'affordability' of expenditure on housing which was raised in outline form in Chapter 2. In thinking of this question, two tenure categories – owners with a mortgage and private renters – are of primary interest since they have substantial exposure to the two main expenditure items of interest, mortgage and rent payments. Of the other two tenure categories, outright owners bear neither of these expenditure burdens while social tenants are exposed only to uniformly low rent burdens, thus housing affordability questions are less relevant in both these cases.

Focusing then on owners with a mortgage and private renters, one commonly employed means of identifying those who are likely to be suffering affordability pressures is to specify a threshold for the share of income going on rent and mortgage repayments and see who is above that threshold. Affordability thresholds as defined in housing policy in a number of countries are usually in the range of 25–30 per cent of gross household income. The precise income concept used varies and the types of households defined as susceptible to affordability pressures are usually limited to those on the lower reaches of the income ladder (see Landt and Bray 1997 for the approaches used in

Australia, the US and Canada). Here we focus on 35 per cent of household expenditure as a relevant threshold, which echoes the threshold of 35 per cent of net household income used to define 'affordable housing' and the upper limit of local authority mortgage burdens for tenant purchasers in Irish housing policy (cf. Planning and Development Act 2000).

Figure 3.8 shows the proportions of all owners with a mortgage and all private renters whose rent or mortgage repayments are 35 per cent of household expenditure or higher, as shown by the 1999–2000 Household Budget Survey. As we might have expected from the data already presented, private renters are far more likely than home purchasers to exceed the affordability threshold defined here. In 1999–2000, 20 per cent of private renters had housing expenditure above the affordability threshold, compared to 1 per cent of house purchasers. In absolute terms this equates to approximately 20,000–25,000 private rented households above the threshold, compared to approximately 4,000–5,000 households of owners with a mortgage who were above the threshold.

The graph also uses the classification by family cycle stage described earlier to help identify those house purchasers likely to be recent entrants into the housing market and thus most likely to have high mortgage repayments. Looking at the proportions above the threshold across the stages of the family cycle, owners with a mortgage who were in the earliest stage of the cycle (households headed by a young single person) had a higher proportion exceeding the affordability threshold than those in most other stages. Even then, though, this proportion amounted to only 4 per cent and was far below the level of both private renters as a whole and of private renters in the young single family cycle stage. (The numbers of both private renters and mortgage holders who were in the later stages of the family cycle were small, so that the affordability measures for these groups are based on small sample numbers and should be interpreted with caution).

Figure 3.8 Percentage of owners with mortgage and private renters with more than 35 per cent of expenditure going on mortgage/rent by family cycle

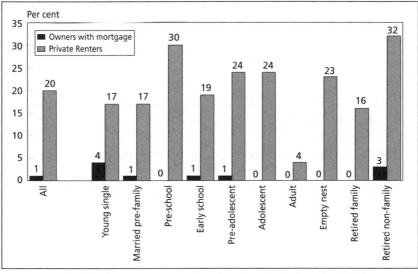

Source: Household Budget Survey 1999–2000 micro-data. For family cycle definitions see Figure 3.7.

3.5 URBAN-RURAL DIFFERENCES

A final issue worth briefly noting here is that of urban-rural differences in housing expenditures and affordability. House prices in urban areas, especially in Dublin, have long been higher than the country average. The Dublin differential narrowed in the first half of the 1990s, widened in the second half of the 1990s and had begun to narrow again in the period 2000–2 (Table 3.2). The question arises here as to whether the consistently higher house prices in Dublin may have given rise to particular afford-ability problems for households in the Dublin area.

Table 3.2 House price indices for Dublin, Cork and areas outside the five main cities (whole country = 100)

	Whole country	Dublin	Cork	Areas outside 5 main cities
2002	100	129	93	91
2000	100	131	98	91
1995	100	111	98	92
1990	100	123	93	85

Source: Annual Housing Statistics Bulletins (various years)

Table 3.3 examines this issue by comparing various housing expenditure and affordability indicators for Dublin and other areas of the country. Looking first at owners with a mortgage, the data shows that weekly mortgage payments are somewhat higher in Dublin in absolute terms than in rural or other urban areas, but are more or less even across all areas when expressed as a share of total household expenditure. If we take expenditures on mortgages that exceed 35 per cent of total household expenditure as an indicator of possible financial strain arising from mortgage burdens, then the level of such strain is low in Dublin (at 1.2 per cent of those with mortgages), as it is in other areas. By these measures, therefore, the burden of mortgages on those purchasing their homes is no greater in Dublin than in other parts of the country and is modest overall. Of course, it is possible that market selection serves to even out house price burdens across areas – those in the Dublin area who cannot afford Dublin house prices move to less expensive areas and either commute to their jobs in Dublin or change jobs. In these instances, the cost of commuting could be considered as a part of the overall cost of housing.

In the private rented sector the Dublin differential is larger in absolute terms, especially compared to rural areas. Dublin rents are double those of rural areas in absolute terms and this carries over into a larger relative burden. Dublin rents in the private rented sector on average absorb 27 per cent of household

Table 3.3 Housing expenditure and affordability indicators in rural and urban areas

	Rural	Dublin	Other cities/towns classified by population size		
			> 20,000	30,000–20,000	< 3,000
Owners with mortgage					
Weekly mortgage (€)	64.0	83.0	78.0	70.0	71.0
Weekly mortgage as per cent of household expenditure	10.0	12.0	11.0	11.0	12.0
Per cent of households over 35 per cent threshold	0.5	1.2	1.7	0.3	1.4
Private renters					
Weekly rent (€)	78.0	155.0	134.0	108.0	90.0
Weekly rent as per cent of household expenditure	20.0	27.0	25.0	23.0	26.0
Per cent of households over 35 per cent threshold	12.0	26.0	20.0	17.0	25.0
Social renters					
Weekly rent (€)	24.0	23.0	21.0	23.0	19.0
Weekly rent as per cent of household expenditure	9.0	10.0	9.0	9.0	9.0
Per cent of households over 35 per cent threshold	0.0	1.0	1.0	0.0	0.0
Tenure distribution					
Owners without mortgage	61.6	37.3	35.7	42.8	50.8
Owners with mortgage	28.4	40.9	38.4	36.8	33.2
Private rent	3.1	12.3	14.6	11.0	6.1
Public rent	5.8	8.6	10.6	8.8	8.6
Rent free	1.2	0.9	0.6	0.6	1.3
Total	100.0	100.0	100.0	100.0	100.0
Row per cent of households	35.7	27.4	16.2	17.4	3.2

Source: 1999–2000 Household Budget Survey micro-data

expenditure, compared to 20 per cent in rural areas. In Dublin, 26 per cent of private renting households have rent burdens which exceed the 35 per cent threshold of household expenditure, compared to 12 per cent in rural areas. Private renters in other towns and cities with a population in excess of 20,000 generally occupy an intermediate position on these indicators between Dublin and rural areas.

Social rents show the lowest urban-rural differences. Social rents in Dublin are actually marginally lower in absolute terms than in rural areas, but there is little difference across areas in social rents as a percentage of household expenditure and almost no social tenants exceed the 35 per cent threshold of household expenditure on rents.

To summarise, urban-rural differences in house prices and housing expenditures operate to the particular disadvantage of renters in the private rented sector in urban areas, especially Dublin. Private renters in Dublin spend the highest share of total household outgoings on housing costs and have the highest risk of experiencing significant financial strain arising from those costs. House purchasers in the Dublin area face higher mortgage payments than do house purchasers in other areas, but these are in proportion to their higher incomes.

3.6 CONCLUSION

This chapter has shown that the largest increases in household expenditures on housing since the 1980s have occurred in the private rented sector. By 1999–2000, the average private rent was almost three times greater than it had been in 1987 in real terms, while the share of household expenditure absorbed by rent among private renters had increased 1.7 times (from 12.5 per cent to 21 per cent of household expenditure). Increases in mortgage payments for house purchasers were more limited: in absolute terms they increased by 42 per cent between 1987 and 1999–2000, but as a share of household expenditure they remained more or less stable at around 10 per cent of household expenditure. For those in social rented accommodation, housing expenditures have been low and stable over the long term and have shown little real change in recent years.

The differential in housing expenditure burdens between private renters and house purchasers is evident across urban and rural areas. In fact, the main negative affordability effects of the higher level of house prices in Dublin arises for tenants in the private rented sector rather than for those purchasing their homes.

From the evidence presented here (echoing the point already made in Chapter 2), it would appear that even for new entrants to the housing market in the late 1990s the increase in mortgage burdens was limited. House purchasers in the early stages of family formation in 1999–2000, many of whom were likely to be recent purchasers, had higher mortgage payments than those who were further on in the family cycle. However, expressed as a share of total household expenditure, the extent of that 'extra' burden on younger house purchasers was only marginally higher in 1999–2000 than it had been in 1994–5 and still left younger house purchasers with mortgage payment burdens that were reasonably manageable and were lower (relative to household income) than the rent burdens faced by private renters.

These developments mean that a large gap has opened up between the burden of housing expenditures for private renters and mortgage purchasers. In 1987 private rents and mortgage payments were at similar levels, both in absolute amounts and as a share of household expenditure. Yet by 1999–2000 the average private rent was 1.7 times the average mortgage payment in absolute amounts and was 2.2 times the average mortgage payment as a share of total household expenditure.

As a result, the most serious affordability problems in the Irish housing system arise in the private rented sector. If we take expenditures on rent or mortgage payments which exceed 35 per cent of household expenditure as an indicator of housing affordability problems, then about one in five private renting households had such problems in 1999–2000, while only 1 per cent of house purchasers did so. Even among house purchasers in the earliest stages of the family cycle, where mortgage burdens were heaviest, less than 5 per cent had mortgage payments which exceeded the 35 per cent threshold – a far lower incidence of affordability problems than was found in the private rented sector.

Chapter 4

HOUSEHOLD EXPENDITURE ON HOUSING IN IRELAND IN A COMPARATIVE PERSPECTIVE

4.1 INTRODUCTION

We now attempt to locate household expenditure on housing in Ireland within an international perspective by means of comparisons with other EU countries. We saw in Chapter 2 that Ireland has a high level of home ownership in the EU but is less distinctive in its level of homes owned without a mortgage. What are the implications for the level of household expenditure on housing and how does this vary across tenure types elsewhere? We explore this comparative perspective in this chapter by making use of data from the harmonised European Community Household Panel (ECHP) survey for 1996, the most recent year for which EU-wide data is available (see Introduction). To update the comparative picture for Ireland, we include data for Ireland for 2000 as well as for 1996. This data is available from the Living in Ireland (LII) Survey, which is the Irish version of the ECHP (the 2000 data for the other EU countries was not available at the time of writing).

4.2 HOUSING EXPENDITURES IN THE EU

The ECHP allows the level of household expenditure on housing in different EU member states to be compared, distinguishing different tenure types. The data is examined here by expressing monthly expenditures on rent or mortgages as a percentage of net monthly income. In Ireland's case, the data included from the LII 2000 shows that, allowing for measurement and

Table 4.1 Expenditure on housing (rent and mortgage payments) for households in 14 EU countries, 1996 and Ireland, 2000

Mean housing expenditure as per cent net monthly income	Ger	Dk	NI	Be	Lu	Fr	UK	Irl 1996	Irl 2000	It	Gr	Sp	Pt	Au	Fin
For all households	19	26	23	13	14	17	18	9	8	7	7	7	6	12	19
Excluding those with no housing costs	25	28	25	22	22	27	26	17	15	23	24	21	16	19	32
For owners with mortgage	22	23	22	21	22	23	18	18	14	24	11	24	24	15	26
For renters	26	33	27	24	23	29	37	15	17	22	28	17	12	20	36
private renters	26	30	26	26	24	29	34	24	24	24	28	18	14	21	36
social renters	25	36	27	20	15	28	38	10	9	16	19	8	3	19	37
For owners with mortgage, age group 25–39	26	26	23	23	23	27	20	24		24	28	21	22	20	33

Source: European Community Household Panel 1996; Living in Ireland Survey 2000

Table 4.2 Housing allowances: households in receipt and significance for household income in 14 EU countries, 1996

	Ger	Dk	Nl	Be	Lu	Fr	UK	Irl	It	Gr	Sp	Pt	Au	Fin
Per cent of households in receipt														
All households	4.2	21.8	6.1	0.8	12.9	20.4	17.0	1.7	0.6	0.9	1.0	0.3	5.4	22.3
Owners	1.4	3.9	2.4	0.5	17.3	8.3	2.1	0.4	0.6	0.3	0.7	0.2	5.3	6.7
Renters	6.5	42.2	9.9	2.0	3.3	38.7	52.4	8.0	0.7	2.9	3.8	1.0	6.3	53.9
Housing allowances as per cent of net annual income														
All recipients	11.4	12.8	10.0	8.6	5.4	10.0	26.6	18.0	13.1	6.6	10.3	14.0	6.6	12.1
Owner recipients	5.0	6.3	6.9	1.9	5.2	6.4	15.5	7.7	11.1	3.0	8.3	2.5	2.6	5.5
Renter recipients	12.4	13.4	10.8	13.4	8.7	11.0	27.6	20.2	19.8	8.0	12.5	19.5	10.5	13.6
private renters	12.2	10.7	5.0	24.9	15.2	11.3	33.0	20.2	16.7	7.9	13.0	19.5	11.6	14.7
public renters	12.1	14.4	11.0	8.8	7.1	10.7	26.8		26.0	9.7	3.8		9.9	13.1

Source: European Community Household Panel 1996

sampling error, the differences in expenditure levels between 1996 and 2000 are slight. This confirms the picture for Ireland of stability in mortgage payments as a share of household expenditure which was drawn from Household Budget Survey (HBS) data in Chapter 3, though it understates the rise in rents that emerged strongly from HBS data.

Table 4.1 shows first (in row 1) that averaged out over all households, the share of income expended on housing varies widely, ranging from below 7 per cent in the southern European countries (Italy, Greece, Spain and Portugal) to above 20 per cent in Denmark and the Netherlands. On this measure, Ireland, with an average expenditure on housing of 9 per cent in 1996, is

Figure 4.1 Relationship between outright home ownership rates and average share of housing expenditure in income by country, EU 1996

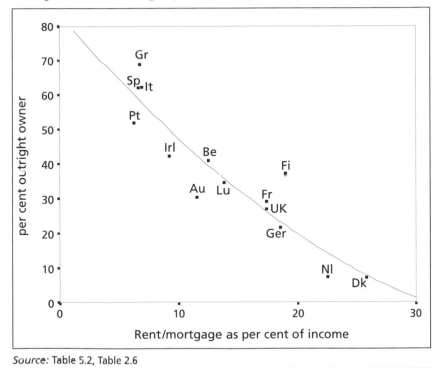

Source: Table 5.2, Table 2.6

below the average for these countries. The main factor accounting for the varying share of housing expenditure in income across countries is the home ownership rate, particularly the proportion of households that own their homes outright and thus have zero expenditure on rent or mortgage payments. As Figure 4.1 shows, there is a tight relationship between the share of income spent on housing across countries and the rate of outright home ownership. Ireland's position in this graph is close to what would be predicted by its level of outright home ownership. The relationship between home ownership and housing costs also reflects the differing levels of aggregate mortgage indebtedness in each country (as shown earlier in Table 1.6). Mortgage debt expressed as a percentage of GDP correlates closely both with levels of outright home ownership (the higher the level of outright home ownership, the lower the level of debts, correlation = –0.89) and housing expenditure as a share of household income across countries (correlation = 0.82).

However, the moderately high level of outright home ownership is not the only factor accounting for the modest share of income devoted to housing expenditures in Ireland. Even if we discount those with zero rent/mortgage expenditures, it emerges from the second row of Table 4.1 that rent/mortgage spending as a proportion of income averaged out over those who have such expenditure was still relatively low in Ireland in 1996 and remained so up to 2000. Indeed, at 17 per cent of net income, the Irish level in 1996 was almost the lowest in the EU (only Portugal was lower, at 16 per cent). This arises in part because mortgage payments among owners with a mortgage, relative to household income, are reasonably small by EU standards, as we see from the third row in the table. Another significant contributor revealed by the table (row 6) is the low level of rents for social renters – at 10 per cent of income in Ireland, these are well below the level for most EU countries, particularly those such as the UK, Denmark and the Netherlands with large social housing sectors. Only in the case of private renters does the share of housing expenditure in Ireland, at 24 per cent of income, close the gap with most other countries in the EU. The final row in Table 4.1 shows that among younger homeowners with a mortgage, among whom mortgage burdens might be expected to be higher than for older households, mortgage payments in Ireland come closer to the middle of the range for the EU.

It is also worth noting from Table 4.1 that a large social housing sector does not imply lower housing expenditure. In fact, the three countries with the largest social housing sectors – the Netherlands, the UK and Denmark – also have particularly high rent for social housing tenants. Furthermore, social and private rents track each other closely – where one is high, so is the other. Finally, in most countries (Spain and Portugal being the only two exceptions) mortgage payments constitute a lower share of household income for those affected than do private rents (compare rows 3 and 5 in Table 4.1). This point is significant since house purchase is normally thought to cost more than private renting, as it entails both asset acquisition (represented by repayment of mortgage principal) as well as 'rent' for the use of capital (represented by interest payments), where tenants pay rent only. Yet we see that the most common situation in the EU (including Ireland) is that tenants in the private sector pay a larger share of their income on rent than purchasers do on mortgage payments.

4.3 THE ROLE OF HOUSING ALLOWANCES

Our earlier reference to the role of SWA rent allowances in private rental housing in Ireland leads to a question about the comparative significance of housing allowances in influencing housing expenditure across Europe. In most countries, housing allowances include state cash payments for both rents and mortgage repayments (as is the case in Ireland, though mortgage allowances are much less significant than rent allowances). Table 4.2 indicates that housing allowances exist in all of the 14 EU countries but vary widely in significance. They are received by 1 per cent or less of households in Belgium, Luxembourg Italy,

Greece, Spain and Portugal but by about one-fifth of households in Denmark, France, the UK and Finland. They are particularly important for renters in the UK, of whom over half receive housing allowances and for whom housing allowances account for over a quarter of household income. Similar proportions of tenants in Finland receive housing allowances, but the level of payments involved are much smaller, accounting for about one-eighth of household income for recipients on average. France and Denmark are two other countries where housing allowances are widely received by tenants.

4.4 Conclusion

Averaged over all households, Irish household expenditures on rent and mortgages amount to less than 10 per cent of net household income, which is well below the mean level for the EU. This relatively low average for Ireland arises in part because a large proportion of Irish householders are outright home-owners and so have zero expenditure on rent or mortgages. However, it is also due to reasonably low average expenditures on mortgage and rent even for those who have such expenditures. Mortgage repayments on average absorb a lower share of income among mortgage holders in Ireland than they do in other EU countries. The low overall expenditure on rent in Ireland arises mainly because social rents are particularly low, while the share of household income accounted for by rents in the private rented sector is similar to the levels seen in many other EU countries. Thus, although private rents are now high in Ireland compared to average mortgage payments, they are not particularly high compared to the rest of the EU.

Chapter 5

Housing Expenditure and Poverty

5.1 Introduction

Expenditure on housing could clearly have major implications for a household's living standards and whether it experiences poverty. At a given income level, a household expending one-quarter of that income or more on housing will clearly be in a very different situation than the outright homeowner with no rent or mortgage payments. Thus, the pattern of housing tenure and the level of rents and mortgage repayments may well have a direct impact on social inequalities, particularly in terms of the risk of poverty. This chapter seeks to assess the scale and patterning of that impact on poverty. The more indirect but important relationship between social inequalities and housing in terms of wealth holding will be explored in Chapter 6. We employ data from the Living in Ireland (LII) Surveys carried out by the ESRI for that purpose. These have provided the basis for regular monitoring of the extent and nature of poverty in Ireland, so it is helpful to start from that base in assessing the role of housing.

5.2 Housing and Relative Income Poverty

The most commonly employed measure of poverty in developed countries is based on a comparison of household income with an income threshold, often derived as a proportion of average income in the country in question (for example, see Callan and Nolan 1992 and Nolan and Whelan 1996 for further discussion). An indication of the likely impact of housing expenditure on the risk of poverty can be achieved by employing this approach, but using income after housing expenditure is deducted as well as the more typical total disposable income. This is common practice in the UK in particular, for reasons which will be discussed shortly. Reliance on income has serious shortcomings, as we will see, but it is worth first looking at what an income measure adjusted for housing expenditure shows for Ireland.

In deriving relative income poverty thresholds, the midpoint or median of the distribution is now widely employed because the mean can be substantially affected by very high or low incomes reported in the survey, in which one may not have great confidence. A threshold of 60 per cent of median income is arbitrary but often used – in the Irish case that figure is in fact similar to the half mean income threshold widely employed in the past. The equivalence scale we employ at this point to take differences in household size and composition into account attributes a value of 1 to the first adult in the household, 0.66 to each other adult and 0.33 to each child. Using this threshold and equivalence scale allows us to make direct comparisons with previously published results on relative income poverty in Ireland.

Table 5.1 shows relative income poverty rates before and after housing expenditure is deducted, distinguishing households in different tenure situations, from the 2000 Living in Ireland Survey. The before housing figure is the relative income poverty rate as conventionally calculated, i.e. the percentage of households with equivalised disposable incomes below 60 per cent of median equivalised disposable income in the sample. The after housing poverty rate is arrived at by subtracting reported rent/mortgage spending (if any) from the income of each household, recalculating the 60 per cent of median poverty line and seeing which households now have incomes after housing that are below this new threshold.

Table 5.1 Percentage of persons below 60 per cent of median income before and after housing by tenure

Tenure	Poverty rate (per cent below 60 per cent of median income)	
	Before housing	After housing
Owner of private housing without mortgage	24.3	19.7
Owner of private housing with mortgage	11.4	13.0
Owner of (former) public housing without mortgage	27.8	21.4
Owner of (former) public housing with mortgage	22.5	24.6
Private renter	19.2	27.5
Social renter	62.2	60.8
All households	22.1	21.3

Source: Living in Ireland Survey 2000

Looking first at the relative income poverty rate as conventionally measured, i.e. before housing, we see that this varies substantially across tenure types. The income poverty rate is lowest for those in private housing and paying a mortgage at only 11 per cent – half the figure for the sample as a whole. About one-quarter of those in houses owned outright are below the 60 per cent threshold, with little difference between those in houses purchased from local authorities versus privately. Turning to those in rented housing, there is a sharp divergence between those renting private sector housing, where about one in five are below the threshold, and those renting in the public sector, where the figure is not far short of two-thirds. Thus, private sector renters do not seem at higher than average risk of income poverty, but public sector renters certainly do – and it is relative to public but not private renters that owner occupiers appear advantaged.

These conventional relative income poverty rates take no account of differences across the groups in the housing expenditure they incur. Simply subtracting housing expenditure from income and reassessing living standards and poverty status in

57

terms of income after housing is undoubtedly a crude approach. It ignores the fact that people on a similar income may simply make different choices about how much to spend on housing versus other goods and services: higher housing expenditure may be associated with higher-quality housing. However, it does give some indication of the potential scale of the overall impact of housing on poverty and how different types of household are affected. For this reason, Britain, for example, regularly produces such statistics on the numbers below average income both before and after housing expenditure – in effect assuming that neither gives the full picture and that the truth probably lies somewhere in between.

We can see from Table 5.1 that taking housing expenditure into account in this way makes very little difference to the overall number falling below the relative income threshold – 21 versus 22 per cent. This corresponds to the results of a similar before versus after housing comparison carried out with household survey data for Ireland from 1987, reported in Callan *et al.* (1989).

In contrast, the gap between overall relative income poverty rates before and after housing expenditure is substantial in Britain, with the latter (using the 60 per cent of median threshold) as much as 6 percentage points higher than the more conventional measure (Department of Work and Pensions 2002). This particularly reflects the fact that most low-income households now have to pay (close to) market rates for their housing in Britain and receive direct cash transfers to support that spending, rather than having in effect subsidised housing with lower transfers, as used to be the norm. The greater importance of housing-related transfers in the UK thus helps explain the prominence given to the treatment of housing in measuring poverty there (see also data on housing allowances in Chapter 4). Housing-related social security transfers, most importantly the Housing Benefit, account for almost one-quarter of total social security spending in Britain, compared with about 3 per cent in Ireland. Including such benefits in household income while taking no account of corresponding housing expenditure, as conventional in measuring poverty elsewhere, is thus seen as particularly problematic in Britain.

Returning once more to Table 5.1, we also see that focusing on income after housing also makes little difference to the very high poverty rate of public renters, which is still over 60 per cent. This is unsurprising given that we saw earlier that housing expenditures are in fact relatively low for that group. The fact that their poverty risk is so much higher than other households is attributable to their socio-economic and demographic profile, and indeed to the fact that it is disadvantaged households which are likely to find themselves in what is an increasingly residualised public rented sector.

However, the differences between the other tenure categories in relative income poverty rates are somewhat reduced when we focus on income after housing. As might be expected, the largest impact is on private renters since housing accounts for such a large share of their expenditure: their relative income poverty rate rises from 19 to 28 per cent. The absence of expenditure on housing means that the position of outright owners (both of private and formerly public housing) improves, and they now have about 20 per cent below the relative income poverty threshold. On the other hand, the income poverty rate rises for those in owner-occupied housing with a mortgage, but this impact turns out to be marginal for those in private housing. Their poverty rate goes up by only 1.5 percentage points, and at 13 per cent is still well below average. While this group has significant housing expenditure, most households with a mortgage are clearly not on incomes in the region of the 60 per cent threshold, so the shift from income before to income after housing makes little difference to the poverty rate for those in owner-occupied housing.

5.3 IMPACT ON THE PATTERN OF INCOME POVERTY RISK

Shifting to an income after housing basis thus makes effectively no difference to the overall numbers falling below relative income poverty lines in the Irish case. It also has quite a limited impact on the pattern of risk across tenure categories, which is where we would expect any impact to be most obvious. It is not surprising, then, to find that the effect on the variation in risk across types of households distinguished in other ways, notably by household composition type or labour force status, is also quite limited. This can be seen by comparing income poverty risk after housing in 2000 for various sub-groups in the 2000 Living in Ireland sample with corresponding figures using income before housing, presented in Nolan *et al.* (2002).

We look first at the pattern of risk when households are categorised in terms of household size and composition. Table 5.2 shows that the pattern of poverty risk is generally very similar whether income before or after housing is used. However, focusing on income after housing does produce an increase in income poverty risk for lone-parent households, from 47 per cent to 53 per cent. On the other hand, that risk falls for households comprising two adults only, from 26 per cent to 20 per cent.

Table 5.2 Percentage of persons below 60 per cent of median income before and after housing by household composition type

	Before housing	After housing
1 adult	48.6	47.2
2 adults	26.5	20.5
3 or more adults	8.9	8.4
2 adults, 1 child	15.3	15.9
2 adults, 2 children	17.8	19.9
2 adults, 3 children	19.9	18.5
2 adults, 4 or more children	45.8	46.5
1 adult with children	46.7	52.6
3 or more adults with children	13.7	12.7
All	22.1	21.3

Source: Living in Ireland Survey 2000

Table 5.3 distinguishes sub-groups on the basis of the labour force status of the household reference person. It shows once again that the pattern of poverty risk is generally very similar whether income before or after housing is used. However, focusing on income after housing does produce an increase in income poverty risk for households headed by an unemployed person (54 per cent versus 51 per cent). On the other hand, that risk falls for households headed by a retired person (27 per cent versus 33 per cent).

Table 5.3 Percentage of persons below 60 per cent of median income before and after housing by labour force status of household reference person

	Before housing	After housing
Employee	7.4	8.4
Self-employed	20.8	22.3
Farmer	24.3	21.0
Unemployed	50.7	53.7
Ill/disabled	54.4	53.4
Retired	33.8	26.9
Home duties	47.6	44.3
All	22.1	21.3

Source: Living in Ireland Survey 2000

Perhaps the most striking difference is in the position of older people. Table 5.4 shows that there is little difference in the proportion of children or adults aged 18–64 falling below the income threshold before versus after housing. However, the percentage of persons aged 65 or more below such a threshold is 43 per cent with the conventional before housing income measure, but falls to 34 per cent using income after housing expenditure.

Table 5.4 Percentage of persons below 60 per cent of median income poverty line before and after housing by age

	Before housing	After housing
Adults	21.0	19.7
aged 18–64	16.9	17.1
aged 65 or more	43.3	33.9
Children (aged under 18)	24.9	25.5

Source: Living in Ireland Survey 2000

Table 5.5 shows that this means that the percentage of women aged 65 or over below the income threshold falls from 49 per cent before housing costs to 41 per cent after housing costs.

Table 5.5 Percentage of persons below 60 per cent of median income before and after housing costs by gender and age, adults

	Before housing		After housing	
	Men	Women	Men	Women
All adults	18.7	23.2	17.1	22.2
aged 18–64	16.0	17.8	15.8	18.3
aged 65 or more	35.5	49.2	25.0	40.6

Source: Living in Ireland Survey 2000

These changes in risk profile reflect the composition of the groups that are below the income threshold after housing but above it before housing and vice versa, which comprise 7 per cent and 8 per cent of persons below these lines, respectively. If we focus on those who are below the income threshold after but not before housing expenditure as a group, which might be 'missed' by conventional income poverty measures, they are predominantly young (71 per cent are in households where the reference person is aged 35 or less and only 2 per cent in ones where he or she is aged 65 or over) and in the workforce rather than retired. About one in three in this group are in rented accommodation, which is well above the national average, but this still means that two-thirds are owner occupiers with mortgage costs.

Support for the notion that this group should not be ignored is provided by their subjective assessments of the burden their housing expenditure represents, which were probed directly in the Living in Ireland Survey. Households in the survey were asked whether they would say that their total housing costs – rent, mortgage, repairs and utilities – were 'a heavy burden', 'somewhat of a burden' or 'no burden at all'. We can first contrast the households above the 60 per cent relative income threshold both before and after housing, where only 12 per cent said these costs were a heavy burden, with those below that threshold both before and after housing expenditure, where 28 per cent gave that response. Against that background we find that 16 per cent of those below the threshold before but above it after housing said they represented a heavy burden, whereas more than one-third of those below the threshold after housing costs but above it before gave that response.

At least some of the latter do clearly face particular problems in relation to housing expenditure and we can see the extent to which this has an impact on their capacity to meet other needs by using direct information on deprivation levels also obtained in the Living in Ireland Surveys. At this stage we focus on items such as a telephone, a car, central heating, leisure activities and an annual holiday – a set of nine items capturing what has been labelled 'secondary deprivation' in previous work (see Nolan and Whelan 1996 for a detailed discussion). The mean score on a summary deprivation scale based on these items of the group below the 60 per cent income threshold after but not before housing, at 0.64, is almost as high as the 0.70 seen for those below the threshold both before and after housing. Those below before but not after housing, by contrast, have a lower mean score of 0.41.

Table 5.6 Mean secondary deprivation score for persons below 60 per cent of median income poverty line after housing by tenure

Tenure	Mean
Owner without mortgage	0.36
Owner with mortgage	0.31
Tenant-purchaser without mortgage	0.66
Tenant-purchaser with mortgage	0.64
Social renter	1.19
Private renter	1.87

Source: Living in Ireland Survey 2000

Table 5.6 shows that among all those falling below the 60 per cent income threshold after deducting housing expenditure, the reported levels of secondary deprivation vary substantially by tenure. We see that among this group as a whole, the position of owner occupiers of private housing – whether with or without mortgages to service – is relatively favourable. Their mean secondary deprivation scores are only half those of households that have purchased or are purchasing local authority housing. Those currently renting local authority housing have mean scores that are much higher again, but the truly distinctive group is those in private sector rental housing. Their mean deprivation score, at almost 1.9, is about five times that of the owner occupiers below the income threshold.

5.4 HOUSING AND 'CONSISTENT' POVERTY

These results firmly point our attention towards those on low income in private rented accommodation as a group to be concerned about. They also serve to illustrate the more general points emphasised repeatedly in previous ESRI work about the hazards of relying on income on its own in measuring poverty and the value of taking directly observed levels of deprivation into account (for example, see Callan, Nolan and Whelan 1993).

Poverty is widely conceptualised in terms of exclusion from the life of society due to lack of resources and so involves various forms of what that society would regard as serious deprivation (Townsend 1979). A definition of poverty in these terms has been enshrined in the National Anti-Poverty Strategy (NAPS 1997, 1999). Simply seeing that someone is below a relative income poverty line is not enough to be sure they are experiencing such deprivation, as is clear from analyses of data for Ireland (see especially Nolan and Whelan 1996) and other EU countries (Whelan *et al.* 2000; Layte *et al.* 2001).

In that context direct non-monetary measures of deprivation can provide a valuable complementary source of information. A measure of poverty developed at the ESRI identifies those both below relative income poverty lines and experiencing 'basic' deprivation – in terms of a set of items including inability to afford items relating to food, clothing and heating – as experiencing generalised deprivation due to lack of resources. This 'consistent' poverty measure provides the basis for the global poverty reduction target in the National Anti-Poverty Strategy.

It is therefore of interest to also look at whether taking housing expenditure directly into account makes any difference to the extent or profile of poverty using this measure. The percentage of persons in consistent poverty, that is, below 70 per cent of median equivalised disposable income and experiencing basic deprivation, was 5.5 per cent in the 2000 Living in Ireland Survey.[1] If we replace the income element of this measure by income after housing expenditure is deducted, that figure turns out to be almost identical at 5.7 per cent. The impact on the risk profile of different types of households and persons is then unsurprisingly also very small. The risk for those aged 65 or over does decline once again, as Table 5.7 illustrates, but only from 6.6 per cent to 6 per cent, with the figure for older women falling from 8.5 per cent to 7.5 per cent, as Table 5.8 shows. The

---

1. This is similar to 60 per cent of mean income, previously used in the consistent poverty measure, but as already noted the median has more satisfactory statistical properties from one survey to the next.

position of large families and households headed by an employee correspondingly worsen slightly.

Table 5.7 Percentage of persons below 70 per cent of median income poverty line before and after housing and experiencing basic deprivation by age

	Before housing	After housing
Adults	4.5	4.5
aged 18–64	4.1	4.3
aged 65 or more	6.6	6.0
Children (aged under 18)	8.3	8.7

Source: Living in Ireland Survey 2000

Table 5.8 Percentage of persons below 70 per cent of median income before and after housing and experiencing basic deprivation by gender and age, adults

	Before housing		After housing	
	Men	Women	Men	Women
All adults	3.7	5.2	3.7	5.4
aged 18–64	3.7	4.5	3.6	4.9
aged 65 or more	4.1	8.5	3.9	7.6

Source: Living in Ireland Survey 2000

Overall, despite these differences, taking housing into account in this way has even less impact on the consistent poverty measure than on measures based on income alone. This is hardly surprising, since the non-monetary deprivation indicators element of the consistent poverty measure should help to capture situations where particularly high spending on housing leaves households unable to meet basic needs in other areas.

5.5 CONCLUSION

The previous chapter found that the problems of housing affordability in Ireland are most likely to arise in the private rented sector and are much less prominent among house purchasers, even among those who have recently entered the market, than public concerns about house prices would lead one to expect. This chapter has confirmed that the same patterns hold when one compares the broader economic circumstances of these two tenures, particularly in connection with risk of poverty and material deprivation. Private renters are more likely to be poor and to face economic hardship than are those who have purchased their homes. The higher level of risk among private renters emerges as particularly pronounced when account is taken of their housing costs. They spend a larger share of their incomes on rent than house purchasers do on their mortgage payments and the incidence of relative income poverty among them rises sharply when one focuses on the incomes that are left to households after their rent or mortgage costs have been paid. Those purchasing their homes on a mortgage are the least prone of all the tenure categories to income poverty or material deprivation, irrespective of whether one takes their mortgage payments into account or not. Social renters have the highest risk of income poverty, but even they are less at risk of material deprivation than private renters. These findings, then, confirm that those in the private rented sector are the main group to be concerned about when it comes to the economic pressures on households arising from current patterns of housing expenditures.

Chapter 6

THE DISTRIBUTION OF HOUSING WEALTH

6.1 INTRODUCTION

We now turn to the impact of home ownership on the distribution of housing wealth. As well as current income and living standards, the presence or absence of assets represents an important aspect of a household's situation in terms of poverty and exclusion, and housing represents the most widespread form of asset holding in the Irish case. To study the distribution of this asset we once again rely on data from the Living in Ireland Survey carried out in 2000, which is particularly valuable in that it obtained estimates of the market value of the house for owner occupiers as well as information in relation to their mortgage. This allows the net value of the asset after deducting housing debt to be estimated, which means that we can analyse the implications of the pattern of home ownership and its financing for the distribution of this key form of wealth holding. In addition, availability of similar data from the 1994 Living in Ireland Survey is also extremely valuable, as it allows us to compare the situation in 2000 with housing assets before the boom in house prices in the late 1990s and assess the impact of that boom on the level and distribution of housing wealth.

6.2 HOUSING WEALTH IN 2000

Housing plays a particularly important role in relation to other forms of wealth holding in Ireland, given the very high rate of home ownership. The pattern of housing wealth and its distribution in relation to other forms of wealth, such as financial assets and land, based on 1987 household survey data have been examined in a previous study for the Combat Poverty Agency (Nolan 1991). This was based on similar information in relation to housing to that obtained in the more recent Living in Ireland Surveys.

In these surveys, where the household was in owner-occupied housing, both respondents and the survey interviewers were asked to estimate the market value of the house. In addition, respondents who had mortgages were asked about the amount borrowed and the term of the loan, which allows the level of outstanding debt to be estimated. This means that not only the gross value of the housing asset but also the net value after deducting housing debt can be derived. (A detailed discussion of what is involved in deriving such estimates is found in Nolan 1991).

We now present results based on the 2000 Living in Ireland Survey to give an up-to-date picture of current patterns of wealth holding in the form of housing using the household as the unit of analysis. About 78 per cent of all households in that survey had some *net* housing wealth – in other words, all but a very small minority (about 2 per cent of all households) of those in owner-occupied housing had houses thought to be worth more than their estimated outstanding debt. Table 6.1 shows the pattern of owner occupation and the distribution of housing wealth by the (equivalent) income quintile in which the household is located.

We see that the level of home ownership is extremely high throughout the income distribution. Towards the top of the income distribution the percentage in owner occupation approaches 90 per cent, but even for the bottom quintile it is almost 70 per cent. The average house value for those who are owner occupiers is also quite high even in the lowest income quintile, with a mean gross house value of €128,000, which is half the mean house value for owner occupiers in the top income quintile of €244,000. When mortgage debt is deducted, the mean net house value in the bottom quintile is reduced only marginally, to €124,000, while that at the top is reduced more substantially to €206,000. Owner occupiers in the bottom quintile now have on average 60 per cent of the net value as the top quintile.

Table 6.1 Housing wealth by income quintile of households

Income quintile	Per cent of total equivalised income	Per cent owner occupier	Mean house values of owner occupiers (€, 000s)		Net value as per cent of gross	Per cent of total housing wealth
			Gross	Net		
Bottom	7.3	69.6	128.3	124.1	96.7	15.2
2	11.3	80.6	138.2	130.6	94.5	16.1
3	17.0	87.3	169.1	156.0	92.3	19.2
4	23.8	88.7	218.9	198.1	90.5	24.3
Top	40.7	87.0	244.0	205.7	84.3	25.3

Source: Living in Ireland Survey 2000

The variation in home ownership rates and in the net asset which the house represents combine to produce the distribution of housing wealth by (equivalent) income quintile, also shown in the table. We see that the bottom income quintile has 15 per cent of total net housing wealth, while the top income quintile has 25 per cent. While unequal, this is rather closer to a uniform distribution across the income quintiles than we see for income itself, where the bottom quintile has only 7.3 per cent of total disposable income and the top quintile has 41 per cent. In other words, some of those on relatively low incomes are much less disadvantaged with respect to housing wealth than they are with respect to income, even though they have a somewhat smaller share of housing wealth than they ought to in strict proportional terms. In thinking about social inequalities more generally, then, it is important to have a comprehensive picture going beyond the distribution of income to incorporate housing wealth (and indeed other forms of wealth holding beyond the scope of this paper).

Table 6.2 shows the distribution of housing wealth by the age of the household reference person. This helps to shed light on the relationship between housing wealth and income in that it highlights the links between income and housing patterns on the one hand and life cycle stage on the other. Young households (those headed by a person aged under 35) have a bigger share of income than housing wealth: they have over 25 per cent of total income but only 14 per cent of net housing wealth.

Table 6.2 Housing wealth by age

Age group	Per cent of total equivalised income	Per cent owner occupier	Mean house values of owner occupiers (€, 000s)		Net value as per cent of gross	Per cent of total housing wealth
			Gross	Net		
Under 35	25.4	56.7	164.9	109.3	66	14.1
35–44	20.0	86.9	186.3	158.4	85	19.4
45–54	21.7	88.0	206.7	189.1	92	23.9
55–64	15.0	88.5	175.8	172.2	98	16.8
65–74	10.7	95.0	181.2	180.8	100	14.7
75 and over	7.3	91.1	161.9	160.6	99	11.0

Source: Living in Ireland Survey 2000

Older households are in the opposite situation. Those aged 65–74 have 11 per cent of income compared to 15 per cent of housing wealth, while those aged 75 and over have 7 per cent of income and 11 per cent of housing wealth. For households in the intermediate age ranges, i.e. ages 35–64, there is less divergence between their shares of income and housing wealth, but even here there is a slight tendency for the balance between income and housing wealth to shift in favour of housing wealth as age increases. In other words, these patterns indicate that housing wealth tends to accumulate as age increases whereas income does not, at least when it comes to the divide between active working life and retirement. Housing wealth thus offsets to a certain degree the inequalities in current income because it is most concentrated on older people, who have low incomes, and

71

least concentrated on younger people, who have higher incomes.

It is worth noting the factors which account for the relatively low level of housing wealth among the younger households, i.e. those aged under 35. First, though their level of home ownership is high by international standards (at 57 per cent), it is substantially lower than that of older age groups. Second, their houses on average are worth less than those of all the other age groups, except those aged 75 and over. This may indicate the prevalence of relatively low-cost starter homes among younger households. Third, younger households have higher levels of mortgage debt on the houses they own – on average they own only 66 per cent of the equity, compared to virtually 100 per cent equity ownership among older people. It might be thought that 66 per cent equity ownership is quite high among household heads aged under 35 since they would not be old enough to have cleared a significant proportion of mortgage debt (keeping in mind the capital amortisation is slight in the early years of a mortgage). However, the house price boom of 1995–2000 is significant in this context since it dramatically altered loan to value ratios among existing mortgage holders (and outright owners), thus bestowing them with large windfall gains in equity values.

6.3 HOUSING WEALTH IN 2000 VS. 1994

It is particularly useful in this context to be able to make a direct comparison between the distribution of housing wealth in 2000 and corresponding results derived in exactly the same way from the 1994 Living in Ireland Survey, before the house price boom got underway. The proportion of all households with some net wealth in the form of housing in 1994 was slightly lower than in 2000, at 76 per cent, reflecting the marginally lower level of owner occupation.

However, comparing the figures for 1994 in Table 6.3 with those for 2000 in Table 6.1 shows that the increase in home ownership over the intervening period was concentrated towards the bottom of the income distribution. The percentage of households in the bottom quintile who were owner occupiers rose from 64 per cent to 70 per cent, whereas in the top two quintiles it was already close to 90 per cent in 1994 and had not risen further by 2000. On the other hand, the mean net value of the housing asset did rise a little less rapidly towards the bottom of the income distribution, by about 218 per cent in nominal terms, compared with about 225 per cent for quintiles 3 and 5 and 253 per cent for the fourth quintile.

Table 6.3 Housing wealth by income quintile of households

Income quintile	Per cent owner occupier	Mean net house values of owner occupiers (€, 000s)	Per cent of total housing wealth
Bottom	63.6	39,000	15.7
2	73.7	41,200	16.6
3	84.6	48,100	19.4
4	90.2	56,100	22.6
Top	88.5	63,400	25.6

Source: Living in Ireland Survey 1994

Thus, these factors worked in opposite directions in terms of the overall spread of housing wealth over the income distribution. The result was that there was little change in that distribution between 1994 and 2000. The share of total net housing wealth going to the bottom two quintiles of the income distribution fell by 1 per cent, but the overall picture is one of remarkable stability.

6.4 CONCLUSION

About 78 per cent of Irish households have some net wealth in the form of housing, that is, they are owner occupiers and the market value of their house is greater than the outstanding debt on their mortgage. The distribution of this housing wealth, though unequal, tends to counter inequalities in the distribution of income – low-income households often own substantial housing wealth and have a higher share of housing wealth than they have of income. Much of this effect arises because older people, who have low incomes, own significant amounts of housing wealth. Even among the younger age groups, though, the house price boom bestowed large windfall gains and left many with significant equity in their houses. At the same time, there are many households on low incomes that own no housing wealth. Many of these are in the private rented sector and have high levels of expenditure on housing and are likely to be more severely disadvantaged than others on similar incomes. The house price boom of the second half of the 1990s raised the overall value of housing wealth but had little impact on its distribution across age and income groups.

Chapter 7

CONCLUSIONS AND POLICY IMPLICATIONS

7.1 INTRODUCTION

Recent years have seen dramatic developments in the Irish housing market, with unprecedented increases in house prices in the course of the economic boom in the second half of the 1990s. These developments have had complex consequences for inequalities in income and living standards, for the risk of poverty across tenure categories and for the distribution of wealth. The purpose of this study is to examine these issues from an anti-poverty perspective, taking account of the historical and comparative context in which they arise. In this final chapter we bring together the main findings of the study and point to some implications for policy.

7.2 HOUSING IN IRELAND

The overall home ownership rate in Ireland has risen from 53 per cent in 1946 to over 80 per cent and, along with Spain, is now the highest in the EU. The origins of this high home ownership level can be traced back to the rural land reforms of the early twentieth century and the policy of tenant purchase of local authority housing which emerged from land reform precedents. A long and complex tradition of grant giving and fiscal supports for owner occupation of housing has also played an important role. Since the 1960s the support for house purchase provided by low real interest rates and the mortgage erosion effects of general price and wage inflation has been a key influence and may well have outweighed state subsidies as an incentive for householders to buy rather than rent their homes.

The owner-occupied housing stock has doubled over the past three decades while the private and social rented sectors have declined in relative terms. Tenant purchase of local authority housing and the falling away of new social housing construction has led to residualisation of local authority housing, i.e. its concentration on a small and relatively poor segment of the population. The share of the housing stock in the private rented sector shrank significantly over time until the 1990s. Though it has increased marginally over the last decade, it is still small by international standards, particularly given that Ireland has a large young-adult population among whom demand for the kind of flexible, easy-access accommodation offered by the private rented sector would be expected to be high.

While house prices have risen more rapidly than average incomes in Ireland since the mid-1990s, falling interest rates have served to offset the impact on the cost of servicing mortgage debt. As a result, aggregate indicators of affordability show some worsening, but still leave repayments on the mortgage required to buy the average new house as a proportion of average income at lower levels than in the late 1970s and early 1980s. This still leaves those affected vulnerable to an increase in interest rates. The gap between house prices and average incomes also makes it difficult for house purchasers to accumulate the deposit required through savings, though it is not clear that this problem is of significantly greater proportions now than at other times in the past.

7.2.1 Tenure by Age, Income and Social Class

While home ownership rises with income and age, this study shows that owner occupation is pervasive in Ireland throughout the income distribution and the social class hierarchy. About 60 per cent of those in the bottom one-fifth of the income distribution are owner occupiers and the same is true of those in the unskilled manual social class. In terms of age, about half of the households where the 'reference person' is aged under 35 are in owner occupation, but the corresponding figure is over 80 per cent for older age groups. The proportion of owner occupiers who have a mortgage declines with age, so that in the 65 or over age range about 80 per cent of all households are in owner occupation with no associated mortgage.

7.2.2 Household Expenditure on Housing

The largest increases in household expenditures on housing since the 1980s have occurred in the private rented sector. By 1999–2000, the average private rent was almost three times greater than it had been in 1987 in real terms, while the share of household expenditure absorbed by rent among private renters had increased 1.7 times (from 12.5 per cent to 21 per cent of household expenditure). Among house purchasers, increases in mortgage payments were more limited than recent concerns about house price rises would lead one to expect. The average mortgage payment increased by 42 per cent between 1987 and 1999–2000, but the share of household expenditure absorbed by mortgage payments remained more or less stable at around 10 per cent. For those in social rented accommodation, housing expenditures have been low and stable over the long term and have shown little real change in recent years.

These patterns mean that a striking feature of household expenditure patterns on housing in recent years is the unprecedented gap which has opened up between the burden of private rents and mortgage payments on households in the private rental and house purchase markets, respectively. In 1987 private rents and mortgage payments were at similar levels, both in absolute amounts and as a share of household expenditure. By 1999–2000, however, the average private rent was 1.7 times the average mortgage payment in absolute amounts and was 2.2 times the average mortgage payment as a share in total household expenditure. Therefore, over the course of the 1990s, as far as day-to-day expenditures on housing were concerned, the position of private renters had deteriorated sharply while that of house purchasers had remained relatively stable.

While it is not possible to identify new entrants to the housing market in the data at our disposal, the available evidence indicates that the limited overall increase in mortgage burdens among house purchasers was replicated even among those who bought their first homes during the house price boom of the late 1990s. House purchasers in the early stages of family formation in 1999–2000 (many of whom were likely to be recent purchasers) did have higher mortgage payments than those who were further on in the family cycle. However, expressed as a share of total household expenditure, the extent of that 'extra' burden on younger house purchasers was only marginally higher in 1999–2000 than it had been in 1994–5 and still left younger house purchasers with mortgage payment burdens that were reasonably manageable and were lower (relative to household income) than the rent burdens faced by private renters.

This point is reinforced when we look at those with housing expenditures above the threshold of 35 per cent of income or expenditure, a threshold which is often used to identify those likely to be facing ongoing financial strain as a result of housing expenditures. In 1999–2000, about one in five private renting households had housing expenditures that exceeded this threshold, while only 1 per cent of house purchasers did so. In absolute terms, this meant that about 20,000–25,000 private rented households were experiencing financial strain as a result of their housing expenditures, compared to 4,000–5,000 owner occupiers. Even among house purchasers in the earliest stages of the family cycle, where mortgage burdens were heaviest, less than 5 per cent had mortgage payments which exceeded the 35 per cent threshold.

7.2.3 Household Housing Expenditure in Comparative Perspective

Irish households spend less than 10 per cent of their income on payments for their dwellings, which is well below the EU average. This reflects first of all our high level of outright home ownership, for which housing expenditures in the present sense are zero, but also the relatively low share spent on housing among those who have such spending. Social rents in Ireland are particularly low, but mortgage repayments on average also constitute a lower share of income than for mortgage holders in other EU countries. Only in the case of private renters is the share of income going on housing in Ireland similar to the levels seen in many other EU countries. Thus, although private rents are now high in Ireland compared to average mortgage payments, they are not particularly high compared to the rest of the EU.

7.2.4 Housing Expenditure and Poverty

The direct impact of housing expenditure on poverty is difficult to trace, not least because higher levels of spending may be reflected in higher-quality housing. A crude indication can be arrived at simply by looking at the numbers below relative income poverty thresholds recalculated after housing spending has been subtracted from income. This is common practice in the UK, where such figures 'before and after housing' are most often presented when relative income thresholds are employed. Applying this approach to Irish data reveals that the overall number falling below conventional relative income thresholds is only marginally different when income after subtracting housing expenditure is used.

However, there is some difference in the types of people affected. The percentage falling below 60 per cent of median income among those owning their own houses outright falls from 24 per cent to 20 per cent when we shift to 'income after housing', whereas for those in private rented accommodation there is a marked increase from 19 per cent to 28 per cent. This is also associated with an increase in risk for lone parents and for the unemployed, but a significant decline for the elderly, who are most likely to own their houses outright.

The quite small group we find most likely to be 'missed' by the relative income poverty approach when housing is not taken into account are thus predominantly young and have a relatively high proportion in rented accommodation. While it is still only one-third of this group who are renting privately, looking at non-monetary indicators of living standards suggests that it is this sub-set that is hardest pressed.

Non-monetary indicators of deprivation are used directly,

together with relative income poverty thresholds, in constructing the 'consistent' poverty measure incorporated into Ireland's National Anti-Poverty Strategy targets. Using income after subtracting housing expenditure in producing this measure makes very little difference to either the numbers in consistent poverty or their profile, as the deprivation indicators already help to capture situations where particularly high spending on housing leaves households unable to meet basic needs in other areas.

7.2.5 The Distribution of Housing Wealth

About 78 per cent of Irish households have some net wealth in the form of housing, that is, they are owner occupiers and the market value of their house is greater than the outstanding debt on their mortgage.

Both the proportion that are homeowners and their average house value are quite high even towards the bottom of the income distribution. Households in the bottom one-fifth of the income distribution hold 15 per cent of total net housing wealth, compared with 25 per cent held by the top one-fifth of the income distribution. In contrast, the shares in disposable income going to these groups are 7 per cent and 41 per cent, respectively.

This highlights the importance of widening one's scope beyond income in assessing the extent and nature of socio-economic inequalities. It means on the one hand that some of those on relatively low incomes are much less disadvantaged in terms of housing wealth and have what can sometimes be quite a substantial asset. On the other hand, those on low incomes and not in owner-occupied housing have no such asset, and particularly if they are in the private rented sector and facing high rents may be rather more severely disadvantaged than others on similar incomes.

The elderly have a particularly high proportion of housing wealth relative to their income. Even among the younger age groups, though, the house price boom bestowed large windfall gains and left many with significant equity in their houses.

However, a comparison between 1994 and 2000 suggests that

the house price boom did not have a substantial impact on the overall distribution of net housing wealth over the income distribution. The mean net value of housing as an asset rose throughout the distribution, though slightly faster towards the top of the income distribution. On the other hand, the increase in the home ownership rate was concentrated in the bottom half of the distribution. As a result, the share of total net housing wealth held by the bottom one-fifth or two-fifths of the income distribution was very similar in the mid-1990s and at the turn of the new century.

7.3 CONCERNS FOR POLICY

The official objective of Irish housing policy is 'to enable every household to have available an affordable dwelling of good quality, suited to its needs, in a good environment and, as far as possible, at the tenure of its choice' (see www.environ.ie under 'Housing Policy'). This study identifies concerns relating to two elements of this objective – affordability of dwellings and tenure choice.

A key finding of the study is that affordability problems in the Irish housing system are most severe in the private rented sector and have the greatest impact from a poverty perspective in that sector (recent stabilisation or declines in rents in the private rented sector would appear to have been too modest to alter this finding substantially). Private sector tenants are burdened with far higher housing expenditures than any other tenure category and experience considerable financial strain as a result. In contrast, among those who have made the transition into house purchase, financial strain arising from mortgage expenditures is relatively rare and has not greatly increased over time. This is as true of younger households that entered the housing market during the house price boom of the late 1990s as it is of older households. The main concern for recent entrants to the housing market arises from the possibility of interest rate rises in the future and the strain such rises could cause rather than from the current burden of mortgage expenditures.

In addition, there is a concern for those who have been unable to get a foothold on the house purchase ladder on account of the entry barriers posed by deposit requirements and other entry costs. It is by no means clear that the proportion of young households that are in this situation is any greater than at other points in the past, keeping in mind that large minorities of households always found it difficult or impossible to enter the house purchase market at early stages in the family cycle. However, a distinctive feature of the present situation is that the housing alternatives available to households in this situation have been greatly reduced since the late 1980s and have directed those households more and more into house purchase as the only feasible means of providing themselves with accommodation.

This point directs our attention to the second policy concern arising from the present study – the question of tenure choice and in particular the limited range of tenure options available to those who either do not want to enter owner occupation or who are unable to make the transition across the entry threshold. The narrowing of housing options facing such households has arisen from three developments referred to earlier. This first is the reduction in new social housing construction from levels in the range of 20–35 per cent of total new housing construction which it attained in the 1970s and 1980s to less than 10 per cent today. This means that a large category of low-income households that formerly would have turned to social rental housing as their first option (usually with an option to buy through tenant purchase at a later stage in the family cycle) must now look elsewhere.

A second development is that private rented accommodation has become far more expensive in real terms and so has priced many low-income households out of the private rental market. Welfare-dependent households that seek accommodation in the private rented sector can obtain welfare support towards their rental costs in the form of rent allowances under the Supplementary Welfare Allowance scheme, but such supports are not available to low-income households that are outside the welfare net.

The third development is the virtual disappearance of the public sector mortgages provided by local authorities and the Housing Finance Agency as a means of access to house purchase for low-income households. In the 1970s and 1980s, public sector mortgages generally accounted for about a quarter of the total mortgage market and were targeted towards those who would be unable to meet the financial requirements needed to obtain private sector mortgages. Today this source of mortgage credit accounts for only a fraction of 1 per cent of the total mortgage market, so that those who formerly would have constituted the clientele for this kind of house purchase credit must now look to private sector lending agencies. The problems of access to mortgages which have arisen as a result of this development may not be as great as might first appear, since private sector credit is now available in greater abundance and at lower nominal interest rates than was the case in the past. Yet it is likely to have added in some degree to the barriers to entrance to house purchase faced by households on the margins of the income levels needed to access private sector mortgages.

These patterns mean that a reasonably diverse set of housing options available to low-income households prior to the 1990s has narrowed to a more limited range of possibilities at present. New households must either buy their homes or struggle to obtain alternatives that have become either very scarce (social housing) or both scarce and expensive (private renting). In any housing system, a significant proportion of households are likely to be mobile or transitional and so require short-term accommodation rather than the long-term accommodation associated with owner occupation. Examples include young people leaving home, students, those moving to new jobs, those experiencing family break-up and older people seeking to avoid the maintenance, security problems or possible isolation associated with owning their own homes. In a housing system which provided genuine tenure choice, such households would be likely to opt for some form of rental tenure. However, the present housing system in Ireland does not make that option widely available. The consequence is that many households for which rental accommodation would be the most suitable option are pressured into striving to buy or, if they currently own their homes, into remaining in owner occupation. Ireland is now unusual in the EU in the very high proportion of newly formed households that are directed into house purchase as the only feasible means of providing themselves with accommodation. This would suggest that what is distinctive about the housing market in Ireland in recent times is not that so few newly formed households are able to afford house purchase but that so many are expected to be able to make this large housing acquisition with such immediacy in the early stages of household formation or as a precondition for other major life cycle transitions.

While this study has pointed to the concentration of housing affordability problems in the private rented sector as a key issue, it is necessary to acknowledge the important public support for the sector which has been provided in the form of rent allowances under the Supplementary Welfare Allowances scheme. These are payable on a discretionary basis to welfare-dependent tenants in private rented accommodation who have difficulty in meeting their rental costs. As indicated in Chapter 1, expenditure on these allowances increased 23-fold between 1989 and 2001 (from €7.45 million to €179.4 million) and now forms a major item of public spending on housing. In 2001, 45,000 households, about one in three households in the private rented sector, received such allowances (Department of Social, Community and Family Affairs 2002a: 76–7).

It has been beyond the scope of this report to study the impact of rent allowances in the private rented sector (though see comments on this issue in Chapter 3), partly because reliable data on the subject is hard to come by. However, a number of policy concerns arise in this connection. The most general is that the rent allowances scheme is designed and delivered as a social welfare measure rather than as a housing measure and is not systematically integrated with housing policy. It is funded by the Department of Social, Community and Family Affairs rather than by the Department of the Environment and Local Government, and is administered by the health boards rather than the local authorities. Thus, it has no institutional link with the system of housing administration. A case can be made that this form of provision should primarily be designed in welfare terms (for a discussion, see Review Group on the Role of Supplementary Welfare Allowances 1995), but an equally strong case can be made that it should also take housing considerations into account and be co-ordinated with housing policy, a co-ordination that is largely absent at present. The rent allowances scheme is not founded on a general understanding of housing affordability problems among private tenants, that is, taking account of non-welfare-dependent as well as welfare-dependent households, it is not designed to respond to those problems in a comprehensive way and it is not integrated into a general strategy to strengthen the private rented sector (for recommendations on such an integrated strategy, see the Report of the Commission on the Private Residential Rented Sector, Department of the Environment and Local Government 2000b: 117–19). Thus, it is a piecemeal measure that, though expensive for the exchequer, relates in an uncertain way with other aspects of the housing system.

7.4 POLICY RECOMMENDATIONS

A number of policy recommendations can be made arising from these findings. The first is that *Irish housing policy should modify the present emphasis on home ownership as a housing solution and place greater emphasis on the promotion of rental housing options, especially for households on low incomes and in the young-adult stages of the life cycle.* For those on very low incomes, social housing has provided a vital resource in the past, not least because low rents in the sector have played an important role in alleviating poverty. However, the sector is now too small to fulfil its traditional remit in these areas. The private rental sector is also now too small. As a result, accommodation in that sector has become scare and, relative to other tenures, expensive, the negative effects of which bear especially on young-adult and transient households.

From this, it can be recommended that *these two sectors, in combination, need to be expanded, both in absolute terms and as a proportion of the housing stock.* It is open to question what the balance between social and private rented accommodation in an expanded rental sector should be. In fact, it is likely that instead of the traditional sharp divide between the two, the rental sector should move towards a continuum ranging from the present heavily subsidised social housing provision at one extreme, through various kinds of semi-social and semi-subsidised rental accommodation in the centre (of which private rental tenure subsidised through SWA rent supplements is an existing variant), to largely unsubsidised free market rental accommodation at the other extreme. The point to be emphasised here is not that the rental sector should have a particular shape or composition, but rather that it should be considerably larger and more diverse in the rent levels and tenure arrangements it offers to households than it is at present. The Commission on the Private Rented Sector, which reported in 2000, made recommendations along similar lines and considered a number of measures which might strengthen the sector along the desired lines (Department of the Environment and Local Government 2000b). Greater attention needs to be given to the Commission's recommendations and a coherent strategy for promoting a diverse, affordable supply of rental accommodation needs to be developed. Furthermore, the system of rent allowances provided under the Supplementary Welfare Allowance scheme needs to be taken account of in such a strategy and somehow accorded with other aspects of housing assistance.

To point to the need for expansion and greater diversity in rental accommodation is not to suggest that the goal of restraining price increases and promoting the affordability of housing destined for owner occupation is unimportant or should be abandoned. Rather, it is to imply that these latter goals, while worthy in themselves, should not be pursued at the expense of either the private or social rented sectors. Thus, for example, the fiscal measures which were in place in the period 1998–2001 in order to deter 'investors' from purchasing housing should not be repeated. While those measures may have had a short-term justification as a means to dampen house price rises, they contributed to the long-term constraints on the size of the private rented sector and thus to increases in the already high levels of private rents. In addition, they implicitly projected the view that where owner occupation might be in competition for scarce housing with private renters, owner occupation should be preferred. This contributed to the unhelpful assumption that private rental tenure is somehow inherently inferior and socially less worthy than owner occupation.

A further recommendation arising from these findings concerns the concept of 'affordable housing'. As traditionally used in Irish housing policy, the concept of affordability referred to the ability of households to provide themselves with accommodation out of their own resources. It did not refer to a particular tenure. A somewhat different concept of 'affordable housing' emerged during the latter part of the 1990s, which referred specifically to house purchase and related to policy efforts to extend access to house purchase as far down the income ladder as possible. This concept achieved formal expression in policy with the introduction of the affordable housing scheme (Department of the Environment and Local Government 1999). The key issue in this new concept was the affordability of housing for purchase by owner occupiers. It made no reference to the affordability of rents or to the affordability of house purchase for letting. We have suggested here that, whatever the financial stresses arising from housing costs faced by low-income house purchasers, those faced by private renters are more severe. Consequently, this newly developed concept of affordable housing is excessively narrow, fails to address the most serious affordability problems in the Irish housing system and is at odds with the tenure-neutral goal of affordability that is included in the official objective of Irish housing policy. It therefore should be avoided in future policy development and a return should be made to the broader concept of affordability that underlies the overall objective of Irish housing policy.

An important recent measure that reflects the narrow concept of housing affordability is the proposal for 10,000 additional housing units contained in the 'affordable housing initiative' set out in the National Agreement, Sustaining Progress (2003). This initiative is specifically directed at low-income house purchasers and, as is usual in this regard, no reference is made in the National Agreement to affordability issues affecting the private rented sector (*Sustaining Progress: Social Partnership Agreement 2003–2005*: 70). A valid rationale for restricting the initiative in this way to those purchasing for owner occupation is hard to detect. It may be based on the belief that affordability problems are most severe at the low end of the house purchase market, in particular that they are more severe than for those in private rented accommodation. Alternatively, it may reflect an assumption that the strains suffered by private renters as a result of high rents and scarcity of accommodation are somehow transitory and socially less damaging than those faced by house purchasers. Neither view is substantiated by the evidence examined in this study. *Taking a comprehensive view of the rental as well as the owner occupation markets, a strong case could be made that any new affordable housing initiative should be directed at least in equal measure, and perhaps even primarily, at the rental sector and that it should be delivered in such as a way as to increase the supply of rental housing and reduce the rent burdens experienced by private sector tenants.* It is beyond the scope of this study to suggest how the initiative might be designed to achieve these ends (and many practical difficulties would arise in this regard), but rather the point is to emphasise the seriousness of the need which arises in this area and the requirement that housing policy treat this need as a priority.

REFERENCES

Bacon, P. and Associates, *An Economic Assessment of Recent House Price Developments. Report submitted to the Minister for Housing and Urban Renewal* (Dublin: Stationery Office, 1998).

Bacon, P. and Associates, *The Housing Market – An Economic Review and Assessment* (Dublin: Stationery Office, 1999).

Bacon, P. and Associates, *The Housing Market in Ireland: An Economic Evaluation of Trends and Prospects* (Dublin: Stationery Office, 2000).

Callan, T., Nolan, B. and Whelan, C.T., 'Resources, deprivation and the measurement of poverty', *Journal of Social Policy*, 22/2 (1993), 141–72.

Castles, F.G., *Comparative Public Policy: Patterns of Post-war Transformation* (Cheltenham, UK: Edward Elgar, 1998a).

Castles, F.G., 'The really big trade-off: home ownership and the welfare state in the New World and the Old', *Acta Politica*, 33/1 (1998b), 5–19.

Castles, F.G. and Ferrera, M., 'Home ownership and the welfare state: is southern Europe different?', *South European Society and Politics*, 1/2 (1996), 163–85.

Commission on Taxation, *First Report of the Commission on Taxation: Direct Taxation*, Pl. 617 (Dublin: Stationery Office, 1982).

Department of the Environment and Local Government, *Action on House Prices* (Dublin: Department of the Environment and Local Government, 1998).

Department of the Environment and Local Government, *Action on the Housing Market* (Dublin: Department of the Environment and Local Government, 1999).

Department of the Environment and Local Government, *Action on Housing* (Dublin: Department of the Environment and Local Government, 2000a).

Department of the Environment and Local Government, *Report of the Commission on the Private Rented Residential Sector* (Dublin: Stationery Office, 2000b).

Department of Social, Community and Family Affairs, *Statistical Information on Social Welfare Services 2001* (Dublin: Stationery Office, 2002a).

Department of Social, Community and Family Affairs, *SWA Circular No. 04/02* (Dublin: Department of Social, Community and Family Affairs (typescript), 2002a).

Downey, D., *New Realities in Irish Housing: A Study on Housing Affordability and the Economy* (Dublin: Consultancy and Research Unit for the Built Environment, Dublin Institute of Technology, 1998).

Drudy, P.J. and Punch, M., 'Housing models, housing rights: a framework for discussion', in M. Punch and L. Buchanan (eds), *Housing Rights: A New Approach?* (Dublin: Threshold, 2003), 1–14.

Drudy, P.J. and Punch, M., 'Housing and social inequality in Ireland', in S. Cantillon, C. Corrigan, P. Kirby and J. O'Flynn (eds), *Rich and Poor: Perspectives on Tackling Inequality in Ireland* (Dublin: Oak Tree Press, 2001).

Emmanuel, D., 'On the structure of housing accumulation and the role of family wealth transfers in the Greek housing system', in R. Forrest and A. Murie (eds), *Housing and Family Wealth: Comparative International Perspectives* (London: Routledge, 1995), 168–201.

Eurostat, *ECHP UDB Manual: European Community Household Panel Longitudinal User Database, Waves 1 to 5, Survey Years 1994 to 1998, DOC. Pan, 168/2001–12* (Luxembourg: Eurostat, 2001).

Fahey, T., (ed.), *Social Housing in Ireland: A Study of Success, Failure and Lessons Learned* (Dublin: Oak Tree Press, in association with Combat Poverty Agency and Katharine Howard Foundation, 1999).

Fahey, T., 'The family economy in the development of welfare regimes: a case study', *European Sociological Review*, 18/1 (2002).

Fahey, T., 'Is there a trade-off between pensions and home ownership? An exploration of the Irish case', *Journal of European Social Policy*, 13/2 (2003).

Fahey, T. and Watson, D., *An Analysis of Social Housing Need*, General Research Series Paper No. 168 (Dublin: Economic and Social Research Institute, 1995).

Fraser, M., *John Bull's Other Homes: State Housing and British Policy in Ireland, 1883–1922* (Liverpool: Liverpool University Press, 1996).

Government of Ireland, *Building an Inclusive Society: Review of the National Anti-Poverty Strategy under the Programme for Prosperity and Fairness* (Dublin: Department of Social and Family Affairs, 2002).

Griffen, N., 'Current Housing Supply Policy and its Future Direction', paper presented to Access to Housing: Affordability, Policy and Development Issues, Dublin, September, 2002.

Guerin, D., *Housing Income Support in the Private Rented Sector: A Survey of Recipients of SWA Rent Supplement* (Dublin: Combat Poverty Agency, 1999).

Healy, J.D., *Fuel Poverty and Policy in Ireland and the European Union*, Studies in Public Policy #12 (Dublin: The Policy Institute, Trinity College Dublin, in association with Combat Poverty Agency, 2004a).

Healy, J.D., *Housing, Fuel Poverty and Health: A Pan-European Analysis* (Aldershot: Ashgate, 2004b).

Healy, J.D., 'Housing conditions, energy efficiency, affordability and satisfaction with housing: a pan-European analysis', *Housing Studies*, 18/3 (2003), 409–24.

Hills, J., 'Inclusion or exclusion? The role of housing subsidies and benefits', *Urban Studies*, 38/11 (2001), 1087–92.

Housing Unit, *Profile of Households Accommodated by Dublin City Council: Analysis of Socio-demographic, Income and Spatial Patterns* (Dublin: Dublin City Council, in Partnership with the Housing Unit, 2002).

Joumard, I., *Tax Systems in European Union Countries*, OECD Economics Department Working Papers No. 301 (Paris. OECD, 2001).

Kaim-Caudle, P.R., *Housing in Ireland: Some Economic Aspects*, Paper No. 28 (Dublin: The Economic and Social Research Institute, 1965).

Lord Mayor's Commission on Housing, *Report* (Dublin: Dublin Corporation, 1993).

MacLaran, A., 'Middle class social housing: insanity or progress?', *Cornerstone: Magazine of the Homeless Initiative*, 5 (April 2000).

McCashin, A., *The Private Rented Sector in the 21st Century – Policy Choices* (Dublin: Threshold, 2000).

Minister for Local Government, *Review and Report on Progress (Housing)* (Dublin: Stationery Office, 1964).

Mullins, D., Rhodes, M.L. and Williamson, A., *Non-Profit Housing Organisations in Ireland, North and South* (Belfast: Northern Ireland Housing Executive, 2003).

NESC, *An Investment in Quality, Services and Enterprise* (Dublin: NESC, 2003).

NESC, *Report on Housing Subsidies* (Dublin: National Economic and Social Council, 1976).

NESC, *A Review of Housing Policy* (Dublin: National Economic and Social Council, 1998).

NESF, *Social and Affordable Housing and Accommodation: Building the Future* (Dublin: NESF, 2000).

O'Connell, C. and Fahey, T., 'Local authority housing in Ireland', in T. Fahey (ed.), *Social Housing in Ireland: A Study of Success, Failure and Lessons Learned* (Dublin: Oak Tree Press, 1999), 35–58.

Ó hUiginn, M., 'Some social and economic aspects of housing – an international comparison', *Journal of the Statistical and Social Inquiry Society of Ireland*, 20/3 (1959–60).

Review Group on the Role of Supplementary Welfare Allowance in Relation to Housing, *Report to Minister for Social Welfare* (Dublin: Stationery Office, 1995).

Timonen, V., *Irish Social Expenditure in a Comparative International Context* (Dublin: Institute of Public Administration with Combat Poverty Agency, 2003).

Tosi, A., 'Shifting paradigms: the sociology of housing, the sociology of the family, and the crisis of modernity', in R. Forrest and A. Murie (eds), *Housing and Family Wealth: Comparative International Perspectives* (London: Routledge, 1995), 261–88.

Walsh, A.M., 'Root them in the land: cottage schemes for agricultural labourers', in J. Augusteijn (ed.), *Ireland in the 1930s* (Dublin: Four Courts Press, 1999).

Watson, D., 'Sample attrition between waves 1 and 5 in the European Community Household Panel Survey', *European Sociological Review*, 19/4 (2003), 361–78.

Watson, D. and Williams, J., *Irish National Survey of Housing Quality 2001–2002* (Dublin: ESRI, 2003).

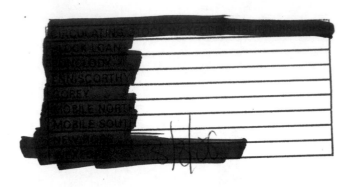